MW01253610

©2014 AFFECTUS:
Undergraduate Journal of Philosophy and Theory

All rights reserved. This book may be reproduced, stored
in a retrieval system, or transmitted by any means,
electronic, mechanical, photocopying, recording, or
otherwise, provided permission has been granted by the
publisher.

Published Independently
Mount Royal University
4825 Mount Royal Gate SW
Calgary, AB
T3E 6K6
Affectusjournal.com

ISBN: 978-0-615-96217-7

AFFECTUS

Undergraduate Journal of Philosophy and Theory

Volume 1 Issue 1

Contents

Why Undergraduate Philosophy?

An Introduction

Ada S. Jaarsma

In the first meeting of our seminar on Jacques Derrida, in winter 2013, the students in the course and I broached the question of what it might mean to study "philosophy" in the context of a university classroom that presupposes certain exclusions. We talked, for example, about the many individuals who weren't able to join us as enrolled students because of devastating provincial cuts to the higher education budget. Several students described the structural exclusions that result from the university's increasingly close relations to the marketplace. Along these lines, we discussed how the corporatization of universities leads to exclusionary dynamics, ranging from the disciplinary effects of the assessment of students (quantifying their work into the aggregate of a GPA) to the ideological effects of the assessment of professors (as sites like "rate my professor" inculcate a culture of entertainment rather than a culture of critique).

The activities of reading and conversing about texts are caught up with market-driven imperatives, we mused, regardless of whether we willingly confront such dynamics or not. Derrida's assessment of consumption explains why we cannot take for granted how we engage with texts:

> The mass productions that today inundate the press and publishing houses do not form their readers; they presuppose in a phantasmatic and rudimentary fashion a reader who has already been programmed. They thus end up preformatting this very mediocre addressee whom they had postulated in advance.[1]

Consumer-based reading practices exclude creative and critical thinking, according to Derrida, which means that the terms of such overly programmed reading align dangerously close with the existing order of values and meanings.

On this account, philosophical study itself risks a certain unquestioning acquiescence to the exclusionary logics of the market. While we might want to affirm activities like reading as resources for securing emancipation and freedom, Derrida's analysis disallows such naiveté. Of course, Derrida's own method of philosophy prompts a much more hopeful line of thought: how might philosophy overcome these constitutive exclusions and equip us with capacities for critique, as readers and interlocutors? And what kinds of practices should we be enacting, both within our classroom and beyond, in order to contest exclusionary forms of repression and create conditions in which critique and freedom flourish?

While this conversation marked the beginning of

---

1 Jacques Derrida, *Learning to Live Finally: The Last Interview.* Trans. Pascal-Anne Brault & Michael Naas (Brooklyn: Melville House, 2011)

our semester-long seminar, its concerns ultimately over-flowed the boundaries of our classroom. At the conclusion of our course, the students moved the seminar into the city, meeting in parks and cafés, shifting the focus of seminar-discussion from Derrida to Spinoza and Deleuze. Students from universities across town joined this summer seminar, which was entirely student-led, and out of this philosophical community came the decision to launch the journal, *AFFECTUS*. In tracing the history of the journal as caught up in some way with wide-ranging reflections on exclusion, I would like, on the one hand, to make the case for its critical aspirations and, on the other, to reflect on its significance as a collaborative and student-led project. In contrast to the preformatted reader, constrained by mass marketing into reading solely along predetermined ways, Derrida suggests that there is hope that critique might emerge out of close reading—for texts that "form the reader" pedagogically.

I see this journal, *AFFECTUS*, as an enterprise that reflects such pedagogical hope. Above all, it was the labour of undergraduate students, exclusively, that brought this journal into being: students put out the call for papers, students from across the continent submitted an array of excellent work, and students gathered together for the difficult work of adjudicating submissions and ascertaining the contents of this first issue. Rather than the constraints that tend to govern the assessment of student work, constraints that can impede rather than inspire creativity, this peer-reviewed assessment reflects the criteria that the editorial board of students developed together. It seems worth emphasizing that these values and ideals emerged out of student-led discussion. In his analysis of the obstacles that often block critical resistance in universities, Jeff Schmidt points out that professors were often themselves the "best" students, those who excelled by playing by the rules. Conforming to institutional norms, he explains, reflects the "long-rewarded behavior that got them [professors] into graduate school in the first place."[2] In other words, there are certain pre-formed habits and dispositions in professors that can reinforce, rather than call out, the exclusionary tendencies of the classroom. Schmidt's gentle rejoinder to professors suggests that resistance is more likely to be found within student communities.

And, as we peruse the contents of this first issue of *AFFECTUS*, we come across examples of the creative, boundary-questioning work that demonstrate the possibility of critical resistance. In their inventive recasting of Jean-Paul Sartre's *No Exit*, "Exit Time," Britanny Burr and Syd Peacock move the drama of Sartre's play from the hellish afterlife into a modern-day university hallway. "Even when I am alone, I am existing with others," one speaker admits, an insight that Sartre's characters are unable to glimpse, let alone express, because of the trouble that this admission would cause for the stubborn individuality of bad faith. It is no neutral declaration, this acknowledgement that I, regardless of circumstance or choice, exist fundamentally with others. As Lisa Guenther explains in the interview with Michael Giesbrecht, the study of philosophy ought to create time and space for exploring "existence, experience, and praxis," putting us more on the hook for the world that we create together. This kind of pedagogy intensifies our responsibility for the shared nature of existence, especially in relation to structural forms of oppression that affect all of us but in grossly disproportionate ways. Since it is the hope for solidarity—a hope that is existential but also pragmat-

2 Jeff Schmidt, *Disciplined Minds: A Critical Look at Salaried Professionals and the Soul-Battering System that Shapes Their Lives.* (New York: Rowman & Littlefield Publishers, 2000).

ic—that emerges from this line of critique, we confront an insistent challenge: namely, to find ways to cultivate solidarity with others, through our actions, choices, and relations.

What is the significance, then, of choosing some philosophical frameworks over others as we make decisions about such actions and choices? In "Democracy Promotion as a Political Project," Jeta Mulaj's careful parsing of the implications of democracy-projects foregrounds the political stakes of how philosophical arguments about democracy are elaborated and then carried out as programmatic visions. Identifying prevailing paradigms as political projects "of the powerful," Mulaj's analysis invites us to grapple with the dissonance that arises from reading Plato and Aristotle alongside a contemporary thinker like Jacques Rancière. It also prompts uncomfortable and deeply pressing questions about what our normative ideals should be for how philosophy and politics come together and how they might inform the nature of our shared world.

In "Rhythm as Logos in Native-World-Ordering," Sierra Mills Druley shows us that our reflections on philosophy and politics are limited if we are not also equipped with resources for confronting our cosmological assumptions. Drawing out a nuanced account of indigenous philosophy, Druley proffers an important intervention in how we think about relationality, especially in terms of the spatial and temporal dynamics of rhythm. Rhythm, Druley suggests, can be seen as "revelatory," prompting a kind of learning that is not literate or visual but visceral and real. Druley's conclusion points to a vision of humanity in communion with "the whole of the pulsing world," a vision that is inspiring and that provokes reflection on the methods by which we might participate in such communion.

Jason Walsh, in his "The Nature of *Oz*: The Cultural Logic of Nature Documentaries and Prison Films," draws our attention to the ways in which ideological constructions mediate our cultural conceptions of life, nature and freedom. While shows like *Oz* represent the panopticon in ways that align with Foucault's descriptions, Walsh exposes how such simulations of reality work to undercut critical resistance on the part of consumers. And while nature documentaries dramatize the plight of global warming, they pacify us with the domesticating logic of capitalism (enterpreneurs will save us) and of naturalized survivalism (there has always been conflict). Walsh concludes his essay by citing a rhetorical question from Foucault: "Is it surprising that prisons resemble factories, schools, barracks, hospitals, which all resemble prisons?" This indictment by Foucault of the allegiance of modern institutions with capitalism reminds all of us who work and study in universities of the importance of resistance.

We will be celebrating the launch of this inaugural issue of *AFFECTUS* with an event at Mount Royal University that has been organized around the question, "Why Undergraduate Philosophy?" While this query is ultimately an open one, with no delimited set of answers, I do think that we can read this first journal issue as supplying some initial responses. Why undergraduate philosophy? One answer has to do with the insights, challenges and commitments demonstrated by every writer in this issue. Rather than closing down debates by appealing to authorized interpretations, each essay advances innovative lines of thought. We can see the thematic coherence of the issue in the very investment by each contributor in the tasks of close reading, analysis, and dialogue. Another answer has to do with the community of students who initiated this project in the summer of 2013. Not content with an approach to philosophy that keeps it constrained to the classroom, these students bring philosophy outside of the university—to the parks and cafés where conversation thrive, and also to this new undergraduate journal. The hope, then, is that these essays will incite further debate and will foster ongoing community, community in which solidarity is an ever-present ideal and in which the boundaries of the classroom remain contested.

Bibliography

Derrida, Jacques. *Learning to Live Finally: The Last Interview.* Translated by Pascal-Anne Brault & Michael Naas. Melville House, 2011.

Schmidt, Jeff. *Disciplined Minds: A Critical Look at Salaried Professionals and the Soul-Battering System that Shapes Their Lives.* New York: Rowman & Littlefield Publishers, Inc., 2000.

Dr. Ada S. Jaarsma is an Associate Professor of Philosophy in the Department of Humanities at Mount Royal University, where she teaches continental philosophy and feminist philosophy. Her current research examines the intersections of existentialism with evolutionary theory.

An Interview with Lisa Guenther

Michael Giesbrecht

Michael Giesbrecht: In a society and culture that increasingly subjects post-secondary education to calculative economic reasoning, thereby emphasizing the exchange value of a degree in the labour market while downplaying the potential benefit of academia and pedagogy, what do you believe is the value of studying philosophy at the undergraduate level?

Lisa Guenther: Audre Lorde says that poetry is not a luxury, and I think this is also true of philosophy. But what is philosophy? Is it the same thing as a degree in philosophy at the postsecondary level? Does it coincide with the canonical texts of Western philosophy? Lorde contrasts the philosophical claim of white fathers – "I think therefore I am" – with the poetic whisper of black mothers: "I feel therefore I can be free."[1] She calls poetry "the revelation or distillation of experience…it forms the quality of the light within which we predicate our hopes and dreams toward survival and change, first made into language, then into idea, then into more tangible action."[2] Philoso-

---

1 Audre Lorde, *Sister Outsider: Essays and Speeches* (New York: Ten Speed Press, 2007), 38.

2 Ibid., 37.

phy can do this too, I think, but sometimes we philosophers rush too quickly through language to the idea and forget the more tangible action. An education in philosophy, or in the humanities more generally, ought to create a time and a space for exploring the poetic dimensions – in Audre Lorde's sense of the word poetry – of existence, experience, and praxis.

Some people find this space in university, and others find it elsewhere. I stumbled into a space like this in a Plato reading group during my undergraduate education at Bishop's University. We would meet every Friday afternoon to read the dialogues aloud and discuss them page-by-page, line-by-line, or word-by-word – whatever it took to make sense of the text. Now, Plato is most definitely a "white father," and he had some rather uncharitable things to say about poetry, narrowly conceived. But the shared practice of engaging with ancient texts and letting them resonate in our own time and place, was a form of liberation from the utilitarian logic of the market, and even from the "credit" system of the university. The Plato group is still my ideal model of philosophical education.

MG: In your recent work on the California prison hunger strikes, you employed Hannah Arendt's notion of a "world-destroying violence," which threatens not only individual life, but also the interpersonal bounds that constitute public, social life, or what Arendt names "the common world," to describe the social and psychological situation of prisoners living under solitary confinement in California's prison system. In an era of world-destroying violence such as this, what hope can pedagogical practices offer, and how can education be redeployed as an avenue for liberation or resistance?

LG: This is a great question! To respond to it, we first need to reflect on the meaning of the world for Arendt. The world is more than the totality of things on planet earth; it is the shared space of mutual appearance and, as such, it is the site of political action. It's not clear that we still live in a world when a significant number of our fellow human beings spend years, even decades, locked up in concrete boxes. It's not just that *they* have been excluded from "our" world, but the *sense of the world* as a place where people encounter one another, tell their stories, and even argue over the meaning of things, has been foreclosed. What hope can pedagogical practices offer in a situation of mass incarceration and normalized solitary confinement?

We can learn a lot from incarcerated intellectuals and revolutionaries in response to this question. Russell Maroon Shoatz has spent over 20 years in solitary confinement and a total of over 30 years in prison in Pennsylvania. But he has never given up on the possibility of a common world and on the power of conversation to hold open this possibility. Even in extreme isolation, Maroon has found ways to share words with other people and, in so doing, to (re)create the space of mutual appearance that is necessary for political action. As long as their cells had open bars at the front, Maroon and his fellow prisoners would hold regular seminars along the tier, teaching each other African history, economics, and other subjects. When the open cell fronts were replaced by solid steel doors, Maroon kept in touch with a community of people on the outside by writing essays and letters about issues that were meaningful to him, such as revolutionary politics, feminism, and the history of slave rebellions. You can read his collected writings in *Maroon the Implacable* (2013).

MG: Finally, it is evident that our common understanding of pedagogy is oriented towards an open future and a horizon of opportunity; however, in light of your experience working with inmates on Tennessee's death row, and your above-mentioned analysis of the "world-destroying violence" of the penitentiary system– what, in your mind, is the telos of pedagogical practice in the shadow of social and physical death when such horizons are radically foreclosed? In particular, how do you view your own pedagogical practices in light of this work?

LG: My conversations with people on death row in Tennessee have been a turning point in my life as a teacher, a philosopher, and a person. I first got involved at Riverbend Maximum Security Prison after volunteering to facilitate a reading group in a minimum security prison. From one day to the next, the Tennessee Department of Corrections decided to shut down the prison where I was going to volunteer, and so I was offered a choice: continue with the group on death row, or wait for another opportunity to arise. I plunged in, knowing that I was out of my depth but hoping that we would find some way to stay afloat. What would someone on death row want to read or talk about? How should one even greet them? "Hey, how's it going?" "See you later?" In the abstract, it seemed unthinkable that we could share anything in common, or that we could orient ourselves collectively towards an open future. But in one of our first meetings, someone said to me: "You know, we still have to *live* on death row." In spite of being condemned to death and locked away for, in some cases, more than 25 years, these men still get up in the morning, face the daily routine of prison life, form friendships and get drawn into petty squabbles. Some become jailhouse lawyers, working on their cases and helping other people to navigate the tangle of post-conviction litigation. Others become artists or writers, creating work that gives others a sense of how prison shapes their lives but does not fully determine them. None of the men I have met on death row has accepted their structural position of social death or state execution. They all work very hard every day to hold open the possibility of a common world, even if that means just a simple, unnecessary act of kindness to their fellow prisoner.

What does pedagogy mean in such a space? This is the statement we came up with to describe what we do: "REACH Coalition is an organization for reciprocal education led by insiders on Tennessee's death row. Reciprocal education is based on the idea that everyone has something to teach and to learn; by sharing our experience and ideas with others, we grow as individuals and as a community." I think it took us three hours to come up with those two sentences. But it was a good way to spend three hours! We try to organize our meetings in a way that lets everyone's voice be heard and that calls on everyone to respond to others in a thoughtful, respectful way. We begin with a quick question to which everyone responds; this could be anything from "What's your favourite movie?" to "What's a moment in your life that you would like to repeat, exactly as it happened?" Then we come up with 3 or 4 discussion questions about the readings and break into small groups to discuss these questions. Each group nominates a reporter to explain one interesting idea that came up in their small group discussion to the class as a whole. Then we spend the last half hour of class hearing reports from each group and seeing where the conversation leads us.

I have found that this way of engaging with a text, and with each other, has affected the way I teach my university classes. Rather than feeling like I should be the expert who guides students in the acquisition of (what I take to be the appropriate) knowledge of a text, I aspire to create a space in which we can encounter the text and give shape to our singular and collective experience. To me, this is poetry, and it is politics, and it is a collective act of making and re-making the world.

Bibliography

Lorde, Audre. *Sister Outsider: Essays and Speeches*. New York: Ten Speed Press, 2007.

Dr. Lisa Guenther is an Associate Professor of Philosophy at Vanderbilt University in Nashville, Tennessee. Dr. Guenther specializes in phenomenology, feminism, and prison issues. Her recent publications include 'Beyond Dehumanization: A Post-Humanist Critique of Intensive Confinement' (Journal for Critical Animal Studies), 'Resisting Agamben: The Biopolitics of Shame and Humiliation' (Philosophy and Social Criticism), and 'The Most Dangerous Place: Pro-Life Politics and the Rhetoric of Slavery' (Postmodern Culture).

Michael Giesbrecht is an undergraduate student of philosophy and religion attending Concordia University in Montreal, Quebec. Michael's primary area of interest is in continental philosophy broadly construed, particularly focusing on the wake of phenomenology and the philosophies of Jacques Derrida, Emmanuel Lévinas, Friedrich Nietzsche and Gilles Deleuze. Outside the world of academia, Michael is a music enthusiast with an accentuated affection for experimental electronic and dance music in its multifarious forms.

Mise en Abyme
Chinatown, Difference,
and Representation in Entropy

Devin Wangert
McGill University, Montreal, Canada

It's all bad through the glass. But we will never get a chance to look. Throughout the majority of director Roman Polanski's *Chinatown*, the spectator is blinded by whiteness. *Chinatown* is the site where vision stops, where the glass has no reflection. The ubiquity of white bodies on the Hollywood screen hardly deserves the title of phenomenon. However, for a movie ostensibly about Chinese—and, by extension, Asian—bodies, characters legible as epidermally or physiognomically non-white appear for a little over fifteen minutes of the film's two-hour and ten-minute screen time. It is reasonable to feel, then, that one has been misdirected by the title. Yet, in keeping with *film noir* form, misdirection is nested. The Asian and the Orient are present as pure quality– a form of virtuality or force. It is quite popular to read the title of this film as a red herring, but to do so would be to wrongly stop at a first-order signifier. *Chinatown* is, in fact, completely structured on non-whiteness. The question then arises: where are all of the bodies?

This analysis will start from negativity. It is through the absence of Asian bodies in the film that one experiences racial difference, and it is precisely this tandem act of invisibility on screen and presence through force that prevents the film from carrying out a simple racist exclusion. *Chinatown* begins by constructing a signified Otherness through a circuit of racially coded signifiers–Chinatown is the Orient, and the Orient stands in for alterity or pure difference. *Chinatown* is not a traumatized psyche, nor a geographic location, nor an ahistorical or immaterial construct of discourse; rather, it is something that derives from the collision of fragments from each of these milieux. In other words, there is no Chinatown, proper. Formal work imposes a third-order signification: the Orient is established only to become a façade, interchangeable with a general notion of mystery. Non-white bodies signify Chinatown, the Orient, but these signifieds themselves become signifiers of a non-racial, flat, intrigue. Being made into signifiers, they are then burlesqued in order to propel the narrative further. Unknowing and a consequent need for knowledge—the staples of the detective narrative—take on a perennially racialized character within the text. The detective's impulsive need to eliminate the unknown has its extra-diegetic parallel in a need to represent—and thus contain—pure difference within a dominant system of thought. *Chinatown* is ultimately a will to truth, a normative urge for the return of the same. It is explicitly about the explanation of an intrigue, but implicitly about the elimination of (racialized) difference. The results are failure, self-cannibalism, and entropy, as the film tries to eliminate an alterity that is its foundation.

1. One-dimensional Signifiers

The film is easily split into two parts, the dividing event being Hollis Mulwray's death. The first part of the work is spent establishing the character of the protagonist, Jake Gittes, as well as the scattering of information in a diaspora that will only gain narrative value much later in the film. Crucially, the first segment is the one in which the Oriental signified is created. Even before the film begins, one is faced with a mystery: *Chinatown,* the title, is purposely obscure and laconic, and the mystery of its referent is quickly amalgamated into the atmosphere of mystery that pervades the film. It follows that even before one begins viewing the movie, one is primed to associate Chinatown with mystery. The film then establishes an array of other positive signifiers—'positive' in the sense that they are legible onscreen through image and sound. Oriental signifiers and a more general not-knowing always occupy the same temporality, with the result that the former effectively comes to signify this not-knowing.

The association forged in the first part of the film is not one of mutual visibility. The goal is not to cleanly represent the Orient—whatever that might entail—but rather to create a confusion that obscures it. The text attempts to bypass the discursive depth of the signified and exploit it as a vehicle that signifies mystery; it does not encourage one to think extensively about the Asian, but instead to associate him, her, or it, with a general epistemic instability whenever they appear in the narrative. Additionally, familiarity with the *noir* genre discourages the viewer from considering the implications of not knowing—for the classical Hollywood narrative promises that the viewer will soon know, even if the protagonist does not. The result is the formation of a one-dimensional signifier– one that denotes mystery through a circuit of racialized signifiers, but discourages any exploration of their content. Temporal coincidence is effectively used here in an attempt to visually flee the loaded signifiers. For example, during Gittes' first visit to the Mulwray house, he briefly interacts with the two most prominent Asian characters in the film.[1] As he waits at the door, a sound-off of fabric on glass disrupts the scene. Aside from the purely unsettling nature of this sound, it is also formally peculiar in the sense that it is presented as originating from center screen, in close proximity to the camera. In fact, the sound comes from a car some distance away. Equally peculiar is the moment in which Gittes identifies the source of this sound. A POV shot reveals not just the mute body of an Asian servant but also the two figures' moment of recognition through eye contact; this shot contains a recognition of difference while also aiming not to cut past an affect of the uncanny. Upon the moment of eye contact, the scene cuts back to a tight close up of Gittes, aggressively excising the driver from the frame. The narrative, at a momentary standstill, now progresses and the driver is rendered insignificant in all senses of the word. This deliberate modulation of narrative velocity attempts to use the very duration of the film as a form of containment. Moments later, the film employs a similar technique used moments later, culminating in the apocryphal line, "bad for the glass." As Gittes is speaking to the Asian gardener, the aforementioned line gestures not only to the verbal obfuscation of information through an "Asian-ness" manifest in accent; the phrase also covertly directs Gittes to the film's primordial scene, set in the actualized milieu, Chinatown. Nevertheless, both Gittes and the viewer find themselves in parallel situations, wherein the narrative accelerates in an attempt to

1 This is a slight overstatement, as 'most prominent' still amounts to 'nearly invisible'.

incorporate intrigue without examining its implications. Just when Gittes sees the 'bad glass', the normative adultery narrative directs the protagonist and the viewer elsewhere: enter Evelyn Mulwray.

2. The Dominant Image of Thought

To truly engage with the stakes of the film, an important digression must be made, one that situates the viewer and the protagonist within a larger framework of genre, mainstream/Hollywood cinema, and Western thought. The latter two categories are in direct dialogue with each other. Mainstream American film typically affirms dominant modes of thought in an act of reiteration, or questions and potentially revises these modes.[2] Dominant thought, as a way of being, also takes the auxiliary form within the cinema as a way of seeing. Thought inscribes cinematic works with a vantage point, one that determines what is legible and what is not. The *film noir,* then, represents an acute tendency within this mode of thinking and seeing, one that repeatedly tells the story of a gradual disappearance of the unknown, the disappearance of difference.

What Gilles Deleuze calls the (dominant) "image" of thought has its correlate in the "action-image" of Hollywood cinema.[3] This is the image of industrialization and its evolution in late capitalism. The dominant way of be-

2 *Chinatown*, in fact, presents a third alternative, which this analysis will examine on conclusion.

3 Deleuze's conception of an 'image' of thought evolves throughout his *oeuvre.* In *Difference and Repetition,* thought is a single image, one of dominance and instrumentality that must be confronted. This roughly parallels the action-image in his *Cinema* books. In his later work, from *Cinema 1* through *What is Philosophy?*, thought is allowed a multiplicity of images, with a similar dominant image that attempts to regulate and efface the others.

ing in the world is one entirely predicated on the instrumentalization of things—the exploitation of resources for infrastructure, commodities for the consumer, bodies for states.[4] This system's foundation is an exchange economy as much as an unchecked belief in universality. Dominant thought believes in a world where everything is already given, where thought does not change, but gradually refines its representations.[5] It is a totalizing notion that attempts to contain everything in it, a notion that assumes all existence capable of representation. Representation becomes inseparable from exhaustion: the unknown is thought of as a cluster of negative integers, constantly being replaced by their positive representations. This image of thought is inherently teleological, validating itself on the basis of a linear view of progressive illumination. The trauma of not knowing is salved with the assumption that one *will* know eventually, or that there always exists in the unknown the capacity to be known.

How this thought thinks is through total representation, the belief in total identification between concept and object. In other words, the proper functioning of this system requires that objects and the subjects that perceive those objects *necessarily* have definable boundaries. This is best represented syntactically: I act on an object. Here both 'I' and 'object' are alienated in space and time. 'I' and 'object' are bounded in visual space through the separation of these two distinct words. They are bounded in verbal space by the use of silence between the words. The easy demarcation of objects here ensures their easy assimilation into a system of representation. This system

---

4 Herbert Marcuse, *One-Dimensional Man*, (London: Routledge Classics, 1991), 155-58. Referred to specifically on the above pages, though the theme runs throughout Marcuse's book.

5 D.N. Rodowick, *Gilles Deleuze's Time Machine*, (London: Duke University Press, 1997), 6.

acts as an inventory that the subject—so long as he or she meets prerequisites of knowledge and power—can exercise agency over.

Arriving at this point, work can be performed retroactively as well. From an outside that is entirely given and demarcated—'objectivity' in a broad sense—one can believe in a whole and static self. This effectively resolves two different subject positions that only contrast on a superficial level. The first is the subject of the 'large form' action-image, an image that acts on a character and, continues Deleuze, "constitute[s] a situation in which he is caught. The character reacts in his turn (action properly speaking) so as to respond to the situation, to modify the milieu…".[6] This is the cinematic correlate of the dominant image of thought—one in which objects and their relations are already given, with the protagonist (subject) occupying a hermetic term within the equation. The *film noir* potentially poses a problem to this conception (*Chinatown* in particular) in that there exists a subject who is not deduced from a given situation but, rather, the only known term of that situation. *Chinatown* (and other *noir* films like it) is elaborated from an extreme solipsism. On the surface, this seems to refute the universalizing logic of the large form action-image; yet, in fact, it starts from the opposite end of the same assumption. This position corresponds to the 'small form' action-image: "The action advances blindly and the situation is disclosed in darkness, or in ambiguity. From action to action, the situation gradually emerges, varies, and finally either becomes clear or retains its mystery."[7] The *actions* that illuminate the small form action-image are necessarily the products of an *actor*. Even if the image retains its mystery, this

6 Gilles Deleuze, *Cinema 1: The Movement-Image*, (Minneapolis: University of Minnesota Press, 1986), 141.

7 Deleuze, 160.

mystery is ultimately given—knowable but not known.

This system of thought, from either end, not only allows alterity or an 'Other,' but necessitates it. The subject is always constituted through counterpoint with what he or she is not. The conditions for this alterity are that it be delineable, though not necessarily delineated, arrested, though not entirely identified. This posits mastery over the Other even if one cannot exercise it. The subject is the child-king, *par excellence*. Alterity functions much like the one-dimensional signifier in *Chinatown*: one uses it as a vehicle to arrive at the Self and disavows it once one has reached one's destination. Language can perform this ellipsis with more precision (and thus less excess) in that it is not required to depict. An author can simply write, "the scene was pregnant with mystery" for the scene to be just that. In the same way, this analysis could conduct a discussion of difference while wholly bypassing an encounter with it. This is impossible in the cinema. The audiovisual image must disrupt many latent differentials that would be more easily effaced in writing. Suffice it to say that it is politically dubious to talk of difference in the cinema while ignoring the differentials used to designate it: race, gender, sexuality, and class.[8] It is no accident that not knowing is coded as Oriental within *Chinatown*.

3. Detection and Difference

Hopefully, by now, I have established a working cartography of dominant thought and its reciprocal action-image within the mainstream cinema. It is through these constellations that the *film noir* and the detective narrative

---

8 This is not to state that these differentials are *necessarily* visually based. It also should not be read that language is capable of expression in pre-racialized, gendered, or sexual forms, nor that these differentials are void of their own resistance to effacement in language.

proceed. This is the genre of difference manifest in the *femme fatale*, the enigmatic Oriental, and the queer-coded villain. Yet again it seems that there is an initial antagonism inherent in the genre. The detective is a character who, either willingly or in response to a situation thrust upon her or (usually) him, is constantly pitted against the unknown. It would seem, then, that these narratives are largely about exposure to the new, and the challenging of thought that comes with that exposure. To the contrary, the detective narrative is *not* one of discovery of the new. It is rather a systematic impulse to eliminate the possibility of difference through the affirmation of knowledge, to subordinate difference to an existing hegemony of knowledge. Gittes—at least the Gittes in our provisional 'part 1' of *Chinatown*—is exemplary of this impulse. He performs his work, first as a middle-class white male, but more acutely as a man who negotiates difference through a narrative of adultery. A testament to the extent of Gittes' consumption by this impulse is that his own private urge to eradicate the unknown coincides with his chosen profession, which does just this.

For all his movement, the detective is an actor of few actions on the terrain of difference. The first prescribed action constitutes disavowal and regression in the face of difference. Returning to the "bad for the glass" scene, the viewer discovers that Gittes is actually given an 'answer' to his intrigue near the outset of the film. The Asian gardener is trying to communicate that the pond in the Mulwrays' acreage is a salt-water pond—bad for the *grass*. At the same time the line points to the murderer's glasses, submerged in the pond—bad for the *glass*, too. This communication is racially codified and constitutes a double-helix of information. Ironically, both statements could easily be incorporated into Gittes' existing structure of knowledge and, consequently, could have marked the successful resolution of a crisis. Gittes, however, brings about a disavowal *because* of the vehicle of this knowledge. As *the* American subject, (the middle-class, heterosexual, white male) Gittes cannot incorporate the communicated information but, instead, rejects it due to its racialized origins. True difference is ignored—the unsignifiable Chinatown that "glass" and "grass" gesture towards—in favor of supposedly stable (read identifiable and representable) *markers* of difference. Visually, this takes the form of a fixation with the gardener's dress, physiognomy and skin colour, all codified as Asian. Aurally, it is the distinction between 'r's and 'l's in the words "grass" and "glass." Through his message, the gardener sketches, albeit in the negative, the centripetal force that constantly draws Gittes towards an encounter with pure difference, but this information is entirely disregarded in favour of a nonthreatening difference represented through audiovisual stereotypes. Gittes, the detective whose meta-narrative is adultery, similarly disavows the information in the sense that he is not looking for a murder. On two modes, then, Gittes and the gardener can speak to each other in English without ever speaking the same language.

The second prescribed action is assimilation. It constitutes another hypothetical ending to the film that nonetheless ends an hour and a half later. After his first and second meeting with Evelyn Mulwray, Gittes has no clear reason to continue pursuing his case. He will no longer be sued for libel by Mrs. Mulwray and his way of seeing has been confirmed: this not-knowing did not question the structures of his thought, but simply amounted to yet another case of adultery. Gittes copes with the return of the new by imposing a view over it that necessitates the return of the same. The unknown is perfectly tolerable insofar as it is legible as unknown adultery. The film continues—or, rather Gittes is continually motivated—because Mulwray's answers are unsatisfactory. This is not because Mulwray's answers lack the objective power or rationale to bring about a narrative resolution. Rather, it is because they are not wholly convincing—they do not wholly *fit* within the meta-narrative of adultery. And that is absolutely intolerable for Gittes—more so than Hollis Mulwray's murder. Unsuccessful assimilation, in fact, spurs an even greater attempt at assimilation, and this scope widens until it disintegrates entirely, thus Gittes' absurd questions that follow Evelyn Mulwray's (false) confession: how did she find out about the affair? Was she also engaged in an affair? How many affairs? How many men?

The detective narrative is a direct descendent of the early Western. Where the former presents the colonization of a geographic frontier and the bodies populating it, the latter is the colonizer of difference. Like indifferent and untamed nature, there are certain 'elemental' hazards that can befall the individual colonizer of difference, but the process of colonization carries on unfazed. An analogous impulse constitutes the *raison d'être* of the philosopher of dominant thought, the frontiersman of the West, and the detective. For the detective, *identification is synonymous with instrumentalization*. The act of identifying objects available to be acted upon is the very act that affirms the subjecthood of the actor. But this connection does not go far enough.

To hold that the film continues past the (false) confession of mutual adultery—solely because of Gittes' colonizing impulse—is to ignore the probability that the spectator is less invested in the adultery narrative's veracity as Gittes seems to be. In *Lost In Translation*, Homay King posits that *Chinatown* consistently performs an act of doubling that serves to displace trauma.[9] King provides multiple instances of this phenomenon within the diegesis, but neglects to note that this process is also prevalent on the extra-diegetic level. This is likely because the dyad operates with such minimal space in between it that it is nearly impossible to see the double articulation. Simply put, *Chinatown* is a movie with two detectives—Gittes within the diegesis and the spectator/apparatus outside of it. This is something denied even by the film's writer, Robert Towne. He maintains that, "*Chinatown*, I think, is the only detective movie of its length in which there is never a break from Gittes' point of view."[10] There are in fact four breaks. They follow a familiar process of instrumentalization and effacement, one that constructs the final failsafe of the film.

The first break from Gittes' point of view establishes the separation of the spectator/apparatus amalgamation.[11] It begins when the detective follows Hollis Mulwray to the ocean, a few minutes after the debate in City Hall. Gittes advances cautiously to the edge of a small cliff and stops to observe the surroundings, Mulwray below on the beach. Cut to a POV shot, prompting the viewer to question what Gittes can see. The next shot *is* a reverse shot and *does* answer this question, but from a vantage point that violates the 180-degree rule. If the spectator were to occupy Gittes' line of sight, he or she would see

---

9 Homay King, *Lost in Translation: Orientalism, Cinema, and the Enigmatic Signifier*, (London: Duke University Press, 2010), 79.

10 Michael Eaton, *Chinatown*, (London: British Film Institute, 1997), 32.

11 It is important to briefly examine this amalgamation of viewer and apparatus. The apparatus includes within it a way of seeing, and thus by extension a hypothetical subject position for the viewer. It follows that the actual spectator at any given time only constitutes a 'second detective' insofar as he or she is aligned with this position. I mention this to illustrate that compliance and complicity are not inevitable.

the left side of Mulwray's face; instead, he or she sees the right. Cut to a shot of Gittes observing Mulwray, again trying to affirm the previous shot as a POV. Cut back to Mulwray, this time from an angle corresponding to Gittes' point of view—yet another affirmation. Finally, in an unmotivated ellipsis, the film cuts to a long shot of Mulwray on a miniature recess, completely destabilizing the viewer's presumably embodied point of view. And yet the next cut returns to Gittes, in the same position as before, confirming the POV shot. Formally this scene is completely schizophrenic and attests to a tense articulation of two points of view, which normally run so close to each other as to be equivocal. This construction is oddly prophetic, anticipating Jack Nicholson's sequel to this film, *The Two Jakes*.

The second break from Gittes' point of view illuminates the importance of the 'two Jakes' in *Chinatown*. In this scene, Gittes returns to his office after listening to a racist joke at the barbershop. The protagonist (framed in close-up with Mrs. Mulwray and her lawyer behind him) recounts the joke to his two colleagues. This is the only moment in the film in which the viewer's epistemic privilege exceeds that of Gittes—where we know something that he does not.[12] In what seems to be a very deliberate renunciation of Gittes' point of view, the *mise en scène* paves the way for the exchange of a narrative *telos*— adultery-mystery is swapped for murder-mystery at the diegetic level, while the former is partially retained as the protagonist's operative narrative. This narrative mutation falsely accommodates the new and acts as an elaborate displacement of wounds opened on an extra-diegetic level. The film comically chastises Gittes' normative impulse—to organize the unknown, difference, under an

---

12 Eaton, *ibid*.

existing structure of knowledge—while, as second detective, retains its own impulse to do exactly the same.

What follows is the first epistemological crisis of the film. It is spurred on, rather than prefaced, by a joke that associates an unknown adultery with Orientals. This scene marks the first mention of the Oriental, and also the first demonstration of its ability to provoke crises in thought. The rapid suture is thus a necessary coping mechanism that displaces the effects of this crisis solely onto Gittes' psyche. It acts as a guarantor that, while Gittes' image of thought and his hermetic self derived from this image may be vulnerable to difference, that of the spectator/apparatus's is not. In other words, the viewer will be spared a crisis in thought because the film allows him or her to exceed the limitations of Gittes' knowledge.

Displacement is imperative because the genetic make-up of *Chinatown* requires that it must acknowledge the Other in order to secure its own identity.[13] As has been noted, narrative propulsion (filmic generation) proceeds through exposure to the racialized Other, and it is generation—narrative at the stage of becoming—that both expresses paranoia against the Other and validates this paranoia. The creative fear of this film is that difference is not a static entity, and this fear necessitates narrative mobility in a series of affirmations that testify to its stasis. Yet it is this same mobility, or, rather, the flowing of time itself, that allows difference to be contingent and protean. Ironically, the disavowal of difference is also its testament. It follows that the possibility of the unknown is also the possibility of a difference that cannot be assimilated into thought. In other words, difference pres-

---

13 This idea was influenced by Homi Bhabha and Jean Laplanche, although what I am attempting to do here is extend it past the constitution of stereotypes and the self.

ents the possibility of non-identity between concept and object, and this crisis is lethal—at least for the ego. The dissolution of boundaries threatens the unity of a 'self' deduced from those boundaries. The operative and generative fear of *Chinatown* is precisely that "I is another."[14]

4. Colloidal Formations and the Impulse-image

The crises of difference that structure this movie are not simply theoretical—they are crises in praxis. Nor can they be strictly psychological, for the subjects whose identities depend on these structures are themselves only terms in a larger image of thought. The *terra fluxus* that we are left with is an absolutely liminal space—not objective and purely theoretical, not personal and interior, nor reified and geographic.

Suffice it to say that Chinatown is not a determined or determinable milieu—nor are its residents racially determined. This analysis has attempted to refrain from citing specific races—Chinatown for the Chinese—for good reason. Just as was the case in the historical correlate to the film's fictional 1940s Chinatown, the actual area in Los Angeles was in no way solely the domain of the Chinese. Its extension did not stop at 'Asian,' either, but included many 'white' Europeans in economically precarious positions, as well as a small segment of Mexicans and African Americans. This explains why the signified 'Chinatown' bears a synecdochical relationship to the signified 'Orient': the latter term is an encompassing convenience that allows the absorption of multiple races under a uniform otherness. It also signifies past (in both a

14 A quote from Arthur Rimbaud. Dealt with in Gilles Deleuze, *Cinema 2: The Time-Image*, (Minneapolis: University of Minnesota Press, 1989), 153 and King, 27.

temporal and transcendent sense) immigration and naturalization by referring to the unknown origins of those deemed 'Oriental.' This is to say that it encompasses a history, even if it obscures the facts of that history.

While African Americans are entirely effaced in the film, *Chinatown* aligns the ethnicities it does show—South Americans and Asians—under the larger sign of the Orient. In fact, Mexico (as much as Chinatown) stands in as a site of unstable and unknowable origins. This alignment is not arbitrary, nor is it an act of reductive racism; it is a historical formation, part of the 'material' aspect of difference. Thus it would serve well to examine the multiple histories of *Chinatown*.

The film is roughly based on the California Water Wars, specifically the construction of the first Los Angeles aqueduct from 1908-1913. It also alludes to the collapse of a dam built by the fictional Hollis Mulwray. This is likely a reference to the St. Francis dam, an auxiliary of the Los Angeles aqueduct that collapsed in 1928. Mr. Mulwray and Noah Cross, played by John Huston, are thought to be two fictional representations of William Mulholland, who oversaw the construction of the first aqueduct and spearheaded the (possibly duplicitous) purchase of land and water rights in the Owens Valley.[15] So there is some fact when Huston's character claims that, Hollis Mulwray made this city, insofar as his historical correlate is held partially responsible for the rapid expansion of Los Angeles.[16] The logic is that Mulholland/Mulwray made the city by building the aqueduct. Aside from an obvious transfer fallacy that effaces real labour, the statement also forms a false synecdoche operative throughout the

---

15 Eaton, 25-26.

16 William L. Kahrl, *Water and Power: The Conflict Over Los Angeles Water Supply in the Owens Valley,* (Berkeley: University of California Press, 1982).

work. Immigrant labourers, mostly Mexican and nominally Chinese, performed the actual *construction* of the historical aqueduct.[17] The labour that Mulholland/Mulwray stands in for is Mexican (or Chicano) labour, and implicates him as such. The claim is of further value because the infrastructure of Los Angeles—by and large, the state of California—was built with Chinese labour. Chinese immigrants built roads and railroads, and later peopled primary industries and factories as a source of cheap labour. It follows that Mulholland/Mulwray, in "making" Los Angeles, are also marked as Chinese. Both Hollis and Evelyn Mulwray shape the trajectory of *Chinatown*'s narrative towards a fictional Chinatown, which stands for their origins as well as their deaths. The Mulwrays, the Mexicans, and the Chinese labourers form a triptych of equivocity as signifiers of the Orient. Further still, the "over 500 lives" lost in the collapse of the St. Francis dam—renamed the Van der Lip dam in *Chinatown*—were largely those of Mexicans working in the orchards.[18] And finally, the orange groves that prove to be such a site of conflict in the film were typically not populated by the "fucking Oakies" that Gittes sees, but rather by immigrant workers. It now nears redundancy to point out that these workers, too, were of Mexican and Chinese descent.[19] Mexico and Mexicans being as much a part of the Orient as China and Chinese is not only a discursive convenience—"gook syndrome"—but a historical forma-

---

17 Thad M. Van Bueren, "Struggling With Class Relations at a Los Angeles Aqueduct Construction Camp," *Historical Archaeology*, 3, no. 36 (2002): 4.

18 Eaton, 26. Hollis Mulwray is quoted here, and the figure is accurate though he does not mention the races of the dead.

19 Laura R. Barraclough, *Making the San Fernando Valley: Rural Landscapes, Urban Development, and White Privilege*, (Athens: University of Georgia Press, 2011), 51.

tion as well.

The film relocates its fictional setting to the late (presumably post-war) 1940s, when both the confinement of the Japanese into internment camps and the dramatic relaxation and subsequent fortification of Mexican immigration policy took place; this process began with the wartime *bracero* program and reached its nadir in Operation Wetback. These biopolitical containment strategies—executive authority used to identify and contain bodies, figuratively with borders, literally with barbed-wire fences—parallel the legislative containment strategies that restricted and continue to restrict American subjecthood. *Chinatown*'s neurotic attempts to discursively contain racialized others—visually, Mexicans and Asians—is no doubt a partial inheritance of its setting.

The final part of the film's organizing legacy is the fifteen years of brutal war in Vietnam. *Chinatown* premiered in 1974, in the wake of the United States' withdrawal from the Vietnam War, and the gradual and ambiguous 'peace with honor' that accompanied its resignation. The work forms a response, a coping mechanism, and an attempt to represent the domestic trauma of a fifteen-year wound, still open. Robert Towne had the inspiration to write *Chinatown* while talking to a Hungarian police officer, who told him that the Chinatown of Los Angeles was a place where "You don't know who's a crook and who isn't a crook...".[20] With the slight modification of the vernacular 'crook,' this closely echoes soldiers' feelings in Vietnam: "You really didn't know who they were [the VC]...you might be going through what they would call a friendly village and, all of a sudden, all hell would break loose on you. You never did know who

---

20 Eaton, 13.

the Vietcong were."[21] Vietnam is the theatre in which representation no longer corresponds to a distinguishable affect, where the milieu of the battle is constantly being reworked. This happens literally by fortification and destruction of earth, but also on a geographic-strategic level, wherein *guerilla* warfare refuses an actualized, fixed battlefront. The ubiquity of its images within the United States attests to an ongoing contestation that is felt *at* home, but felt *as* elsewhere. Vietnam, like the signified Chinatown, supersedes its geography.[22]

It follows that when Towne says that *Chinatown*/Chinatown is "Jake's fucked up state of mind" he only addresses one aspect of its significance.[23] Chinatown, as much as it can be thought of as a space, does not have a corresponding place, or a determinable geography. A cinematic or linguistic representation of Chinatown—and by extension, of difference—can only be a representation of its symptoms.

Much like the fictional/historical dams of Los Angeles, race is regulated and exploited by a dominant power. Chinatown is a discursive swamp—an artificial enclosure created in an attempt to fix the identity of otherness, a reservoir for dominant ideology to draw upon. As Homi Bhabha notes, Self and Other—colonizer and colonized—are both terms within a highly striated system of thought.[24] The colonizer is not outside of the enclosure. Bhabha posits that, because of the impossibility of an

---

21 Robert S. Laufer, and M.S. Gallops, "War Stress and Trauma: The Vietnam Veteran Experience," *Journal of Health and Social Behavior*, 25, no. 1 (1984): 67.

22 Sylvia Shin Huey Chong, *The Oriental Obscene: Violence and Racial Fantasies in the Vietnam Era*, (London: Duke University Press, 2012), 38-74, 127-172.

23 Eaton, 13.

24 Homi Bhabha, "The Other Question," *Screen*, 6, no. 24 (1983): 25.

encompassing stereotype, of total identification, all attempts to restrict discursive movement ultimately fail.[25] Mulwray is prophetic in believing that "cesspools are where life begins." The artificial reservoir stagnates, and in this stagnation the matter interacts, ferments and recreates itself in new configurations. Identities of subjects as much as objects are colloidal and destabilized. This is to say that, if identity is positivistic, a solid in the swamp, then difference is the structuring and deconstructing current that underlies it. This is an image of non-identity between concept and object, an indeterminacy of the 'objective'—one that makes the term a misnomer.[26] It is consequently the site where the self-in-becoming is constituted from alterity, since alterity is *all* there is. Following Jean Laplanche, this is the embryonic stage of introjection, wherein the ego absorbs the Other *before* it projects a self.[27] Finally, this is *Chinatown*/Chinatown, the work and the signified.

The work itself is what Deleuze calls an impulse-image—a dyad formed of elementary impulses and an originary world. The originary world is analogous to the signified Orient, a "pure background, or rather without-background...but it is also the set which unites everything, not in an organization, but making all the parts converge in an immense rubbish-dump or swamp, and all the impulses in a great death impulse."[28] The swamp of this film is one of partial forms, a kind of pre-constitution in which formations are marked with race, sex, and gender, without being racialized, sexualized and

---

25 *Ibid.*, 27.

26 Non-identity theorized by Theodor W. Adorno in *Negative Dialectics*.

27 King, quoting Jean Laplanche, 31.

28 Deleuze, *Cinema 1: The Movement-Image*, 124.

gendered.[29] One sees this background become literal through a thematic in the *mise en scène* that backgrounds the Asian and South American servants in both the Mulwrays' mansion and Cross' ranch. *Chinatown*—work and signified—is precisely this rubbish-dump through which determinate milieu are constituted. One never sees the originary world for it, "rumbles in the depths of all the milieux and runs along beneath them."[30] In the colloidal swamp of *Chinatown*, milieux emerge from the originary world only to disappear back into it, reconstituted again in different formations. One sees the result of this motion in the Mulwray house, the most frequently recurring milieu and yet one which is constantly de- and re-constructed with every return.

The first encounter with this milieu sees it established as a proper—if peculiar—domestic space. Servants are performing banal tasks; both the interior and exterior of the house are well maintained, lived-in. The next time Gittes returns to the house, it has been emptied except for Evelyn. The once shining vista is now diffused with shadow, the exterior shots of the mansion displaying no interior use of electric light. The third return to the house brings with it a total reworking of the space, all objects are hidden within suitcases or beneath shrouds. The fourth and final return sees the house again shrouded in darkness, though this time its very ownership has been reworked. While Noah Cross seems initially to be an invasive force in the house, territory is reworked and the house instead yields two of his paid thugs. It has become a space of death, pre-figured by the shrouds in the third return. This is because the impulse-image is "inseparable from an entropy, a degradation," a pull towards the origi-

29 An example of this (involving Evelyn Mulwray's racial ambiguity) will be returned to later.

30 *Ibid.,* 125.

nary world that constitutes it.[31] This parallels the milieu of the reservoir, which is re-worked three times and finally ends as a space of death for Hollis Mulwray. Each use of the Oriental signified arcs and flittingly illuminates the machinations of the originary world through its own march back to that world.

The supposed façade of the one-dimensional signifier stratifies into the "pure background" of the originary world. The Oriental signifiers refuse to signify at all, or rather do so only with a multiplicity and ambivalence of meaning. Chinatown, the signified, cannot be contained by a narrative apparatus that represses its content in order to extract an affect of mystery. The result in the second half of the film is that Chinatown is re-inflated, so to speak. It again takes on a polysemy and indeterminacy, becoming what Homay King calls an "enigmatic signifier."[32] Conducting a reading of Laplanche, King locates the seduction of enigmatic signifiers in their promise to return to and explain the origins of the Other, lodged at the heart of the self.[33] Rather than her conventional beauty, it is this promise of a return to origins that is the true seductive force of Evelyn Mulwray, an enigmatic signifier both as woman and as Oriental. The enigmatic signifier is indeterminate in that it cannot be solved or put into a circuit—or, if it does enter a circuit, it is one of infinite regress. Eaton notes that Faye Dunaway (the actress who plays Evelyn Mulwray), in addition to being completely surrounded by Orientals—here, Mexicans and Asians—and in addition to having a past bound up in a Mexico codified as Orient, is also 'made up' to

31 *Ibid.*, 126.

32 King, 1-43.

33 King, 24.

look Asian.[34] This is evident in the manipulated shape of her eyes, as well as her shaved eyebrows. She is simultaneously supposed to be read as the apotheosis of white womanhood, expressed through her vulnerability, porcelain composition, and blonde hair. Which reading is correct? The answer is both. This indeterminacy extends to the incest-taken-for-miscegenation plot, wherein Evelyn Mulwray's originary trauma is read as sex with an Oriental. In fact, the trauma is rape by her white father. Above all, indeterminacy carries with it a constitutive immediacy, a quadruple citation that makes it impossible to privilege race, gender, sexuality, or class as the primordial difference occurring before the others. By the time the film arrives at the scene in which Evelyn Mulwray confesses that Katherine is her sister *and* her daughter, the psychological and narratological toll of the enigmatic signifiers is already felt. Fully seduced, the film advances towards the originary world.

5. Bad Repetition and Entropy

The two detectives' importance arrives at the peak of the signifiers' ambiguity. The film clearly becomes aware of its diegetic entropy, but not of the entropy of the Hollywood form itself. This is at the root of Towne and Polanski's argument over the film's ending. Towne wanted to collapse Chinatown again into a one-dimensional signifier; everyone would escape safely to Mexico and the movie would end without reflecting upon those implications. However, it seems that Polanski realized that such an ending would be impossible.[35] One can hardly see a happy ending in an escape to the same 'elsewhere' that

34 Eaton, 43.

35 Eaton, 65.

has threatened to obliterate the film at every moment. Polanski instead follows a final impulse of the *noir* detective: he tries to make good on his promise to show us Chinatown. His attempt proves entirely inadequate. This realization does not come in retrospect; inadequacy impregnates the final twenty minutes of the film…until morbidity takes over. In a film that spans over two hours, it is surprising that what is possibly the most privileged part of the narrative seems rushed. Diegetic day turns to night much faster than at any other point during the film. This is the only scene in which the spectator's epistemological privilege is apparently less than Gittes'. The viewer sees him go from milieu to milieu, sitting on a revelation unknown to them. The evidence of Gittes' knowledge (expressed in close-up after he has found a pair of glasses in the Mulwray's pond) allows the viewer to trust that he is going to execute a plan and bring about a narrative resolution—the classical Hollywood protagonist. And yet it takes only two minutes of screen time for Gittes to be outwitted. He is first coerced by Cross—whom he attempted to apprehend—into divulging the whereabouts of 'the girl'—whom he intended to protect. Moments later, he is arrested—in both senses of the word—by the very institution that he believed would bring about a narrative resolution. That this all happens in ten minutes encourages the viewer to exclaim, 'Wait, Jake—I thought you had a plan!"

This amounts to an affective deferral. It attempts to anticipate and address the feeling of inadequacy that pervades the final scene, pre-murder. It provides a response to an entirely different (and nominal) objection not yet raised, in the hope of obscuring one that threatens to undermine the very text itself. "This is not an effective narrative agent" replaces "this is not Chinatown."

Towne and Polanski actually want to achieve the

same thing with their respective endings—to collapse the enigmatic signifier back into a one-dimensional signifier. Polanski attempts to exhaust the originary world, 'Chinatown,' by actualizing it—thus the set of the last scene. Representation becomes a form of exorcism. In a figurative parallel to William Mulholland's apocryphal line at the groundbreaking of the first Los Angeles aqueduct, Polanski also exclaims, "There it is! Take it!" His gift comes with a caveat, though: he allows that Gittes can be undone by alterity, that his point of view's rationality does not need to be sated. The private detective that is the apparatus does need to have its mode of thought confirmed, however. And this is the true stake of the film: *we* must see Chinatown. All of it.

The scene begins with a series of nominative sentences in the form of assertions. "These are my associates," "I am Mr. Cross," "I am rich." "Evelyn Mulwray is my daughter." These assertions amount to the territorialization of bodies and are predicated on the anxiety that here biopolitics—bodies and their relations to each other—cannot be easily demarcated. Just as this seems to be the case, the film cuts to Mulwray's sister/daughter Katherine—the unstable body *par excellence*—as Cross runs towards her, stating "I, I am…your…your *grandfather*." Cross, not only assertive in his cadence seconds before but also in his ontological status, now flounders, and for good reason: it is not determinable what Cross *is* in relation to Katherine.

In Chinatown, the milieu, sound refuses to constitute a three-dimensional space. Instead, unidentifiable ambient noise overtakes the faltering dialogue at times. The shot from deputy Loach's pistol creates a vacuum. All background noise is eliminated as a horn *crescendos* from a murky and almost material silence. A scream follows. Sound here becomes animal; it is all expression and no communication. When dialogue returns it is against an otherwise muted soundscape. Sight fails, or rather it is no longer part of a sensory-motor schema that extends seeing into acting. After Gittes sees the dead Evelyn Mulwray, a bullet-hole in the place of her left eye, his eyes are deadened, too. Gittes cannot make eye contact for the rest of the film. As he walks into the darkness, the central lighting fades and casts the Asian bodies that approach into a *chiaroscuro* that only reveals eyes, noses, mouths, never faces. This is the result of Gittes' encounter with difference, the racialized Other that he has been pursuing for the entirety of the film. It is both apex and nadir of the normative detective in his impulse to eradicate difference. The film demonstrates that Gittes' encounter with and attempted mastery over the racialized Other is ultimately an un-founding and figurative death of the self. And this is where the film is supposed to end, in a cruel equilibrium that equates the death of the racialized Other (literally, Evelyn Mulwray, but no less Chinatown captured in representation) with the unmaking of Gittes' self. And yet it does not.

Chinatown, like its protagonist, 'does not know what it is dealing with,' and Gittes unsuccessfully takes the fall for the film. In a final attempt to disavow the ideological work it has been performing throughout its runtime, it displaces its own extra-diegetic trauma onto his psyche. The second detective, the spectator/apparatus has, to an even greater extent than Gittes, tried to incorporate the racialized and gendered Other into a system of representation that fixes, defines, and masters difference. The spectator's investment in this film is precisely kin to Gittes' investment in the Mulwray case—namely, that what one wants from *Chinatown* is the affirmation of their own dominant image of thought. This takes the form of the murder-mystery either thwarted or at least explained, the delineation and essentialization of the racialized Other, and the representation of difference, so as to assimilate and explain this force that has been so destructive throughout the film. The film is appealing, even seductive, in its flirtations with difference, but only insofar as this burlesque ends with the entirety of the thing un-shrouded, laid bare. What is intolerable and truly unmaking about this film is not that it ends in the absence of an answer, but ends instead in the presence of an unanswerable difference.

A sense of urgency pervades the final scene. The affirmation of the dominant image of thought amounts to a "bad repetition," a circuit that is held in check by equilibrium between the positive, centripetal force of stereotyping or essentializing, and a negative centrifugal force, a return to origins—death.[36] Bad repetition is not perfect repetition: Chinatown, the enigmatic signifier, depreciates with every attempt to fix it. The film demonstrates that while pure difference cannot be exhausted, the *terra* on which this process takes place can be; thus, the mutating house or reservoir, represented so many different times as to finally depreciate into spaces of death. This sense of immediacy resonates in a real present that is seeing an increasing stratification of class, the rise of fascist organizations in developed and developing countries alike, and the reification of dominant ways of seeing through race, gender, class, and sexuality. It is not simply about identifying the ground on which one can fight dominant ideology, but about realizing that this ground is decaying by the second.

Unable to stop the bad repetition, sate or overcome this impulse, *Chinatown* begins to disintegrate. The audiovisual image decomposes, not because sound and

---

36 Term borrowed from Deleuze, *Cinema 1: The Movement-Image*, 132.

image are no longer complimentary, but because they have no common intersection: they cannot converge on a representation. Chinatown is still elsewhere. The movie's final scene depicts only pieces of the mute Asian bodies inhabiting the frame. At the same time, Lou, whose voice issues commands throughout the remainder of the scene, is pushed out of frame and enveloped in darkness. This 'elsewhere' is further exacerbated by the last one-liner of the film, a statement so sickly inept: "Forget it, Jake—it's Chinatown." It is stated as a redundancy. "It's China-town" implies that elaboration is unnecessary, because it is already known *what Chinatown is*—the equivalent of "it's Vietnam," "it's Black". Only the viewer cannot forget it, because it is not Chinatown, nor is it the Orient, nor the Other: the spectator's eyes are deadened as well. The affective ending does not leave one "dealing with" the narrative-generated sadness of Mulwray's death; rather, the horror is one of extreme ambivalence. We do not know what we are dealing with precisely because what we are dealing with undermines our system of 'dealing': the classical Hollywood system of representation, the action-image.

Michael Eaton begins his book, *Chinatown*, with a eulogy. He states that "*Chinatown* is the last, so it is often said, 'studio picture', a film which was made in a time when it was still possible for a Hollywood major to produce a complex work...[that] is never sucked into the maelstrom of cynicism."[37] The decline of the Hollywood studio system occurred for a myriad of reasons, but the decline of widespread belief in the truths of that system's products is not so overdetermined. The film is not only aware of its narrative entropy, but of the corresponding entropies of a system of production that created it and a

---

37 Eaton, 7.

system of thought that gave it meaning. The image-in-decay is the image of a crisis of faith in the grand narratives of Hollywood and the grand narratives of America at large. It marks a final *full-hearted* attempt to validate the dominant image of thought by endeavoring to represent and thus assimilate into it the very Other that shook its foundations: an originary world contemporarily called 'Vietnam,' but since the founding of the country known as 'race' and 'gender'.

Chinatown illustrates, by example, a third action in the face of difference, one between disavowal and assimilation. This is being *acted upon* and utterly obliterated by it. And yet difference is not the tragedy: the tragedy is rather that we are, from the outset, aligned with the film as antagonists of difference. Like most tragedies, it is tragic because it is not inevitable. So the credits encroach on the motionless viewer, suspended in the air, affected and mute. The spectator is repelled from the diegesis. And at the close, what is disturbing is not a feeling of complicity in the murder of Evelyn Mulwray. It is the knowledge that we have sat, in utter passivity, as the Hollywood system of representation commits suicide.

Bibliography

Adorno, Theodor W. *Negative Dialectics*. London: Continuum International Publishing Group, 2007.

Bhabha, Homi. "The Other Question." *Screen*. no. 24 (1983): 18-36.

Barraclough, Laura R. *Making the San Fernando Valley: Rural Landscapes, Urban Development, and White Privilege*. Athens: University of Georgia Press, 2011.

Chong, Sylvia Shin Huey. *The Oriental Obscene: Violence and Racial Fantasies in the Vietnam Era*. London: Duke University Press, 2012.

Deleuze, Gilles. *Cinema 1: The Movement-Image*. Minneapolis: University of Minnesota Press, 1986.

Deleuze, Gilles. *Cinema 2: The Time-Image*. Minneapolis: University of Minnesota Press, 1989.

Eaton, Michael. *Chinatown*. London: British Film Institute, 1997.

Kahrl, William L. *Water and Power: The Conflict Over Los Angeles Water Supply in the Owens Valley*. Berkeley: University of California Press, 1982.

King, Homay. *Lost in Translation: Orientalism, Cinema, and the Enigmatic Signifier*. London: Duke University Press, 2010.

Laufer, Robert S., and M.S. Gallops. "War Stress and Trauma: The Vietnam Veteran Experience." *Journal of Health and Social Behavior*. no. 1 (1984): 65-85.

Marcuse, Herbert, *One-Dimensional Man*. London: Routledge Classics, 1991.

Polanski, Roman, & Towne, Robert. "Chinatown." Paramount Pictures 1974. DVD.

Rodowick, D.N. *Gilles Deleuze's Time Machine*. London: Duke University Press, 1997.

Van Bueren, Thad M. "Struggling With Class Relations at a Los Angeles Aqueduct Construction Camp ." *Historical Archaeology*. no. 36 (2002): 28-43.

Devin Wangert is interested in intersections and encounters between philosophy and other creative forms. His praxis aims to not only draw conceptual parallels between philosophy and various media, but more vitally, to reach a limit-state by opening these (typically) closed systems onto each other. Ultimately, he is concerned with generating interstices that lead to the concrete—whether it is the refusal of such categories as "pure entertainment," or the forcible grounding of otherwise ahistorical and abstract concepts. Wangert's current research takes up the concepts of duration and image within the cinema. These notions are being studied in their relationship to Henri Bergson's crucial reconceptualization of a time not subordinated to space, and his impression of matter as image. Devin currently works in the Cultural Studies program at McGill University, in Montreal, Quebec.

Bartleby
Agrammatical Resistance and the Law

Tim Christiaens
Catholic University of Leuven, Leuven, Belgium

And what can life be worth if the first rehearsal of life is life it-self? That is why life is always like a sketch. No, "sketch" is not quite the word, because a sketch is an outline of something, the groundwork for a picture, whereas the sketch that is our life is a sketch for nothing, an outline with no picture.
-Milan Kundera

1. Introduction

A lot of philosophers have engaged with Melville's short story "Bartleby, the Scrivener"[1] to talk about resistance.[2] Gilles Deleuze is no exception. He analyzed Bartleby's formula "I would prefer not to" as an agrammaticality that ruptures the functioning of language and the law. It points to an outside from which we can escape the dominance of the law. This form of resistance will be the subject of this article. Firstly, we will give a quick overview of Melville's short story. Afterwards, we will examine against what Bartleby resists. What is this law and what is wrong with it? Thirdly, we will see in what sense the for-

1 Herman Melville, "Bartleby, the Scrivener: a Story of Wall-Street," in *Great Short Works of Herman Melville* (New York: Harper Perennial Modern Classics, 2004), 39-74 (henceforth BTS).

2 Examples are Deleuze (Gilles Deleuze, "Bartleby, ou la Formule," in *Critique et Clinique* (Paris: Les Editions de Minuit), 89-114; henceforth BOLF), Agamben (Giorgio Agamben, "Bartleby, or On Contingency," in *Potentialities* (Stanford: Stanford University Press, 1999), 243-271) and Negri & Hardt (Atonio Negri and Michael Hardt, *Empire* (Cambridge: Harvard University Press, 2000)).

mula "I would prefer not to" is a kind of resistance, which will lead us to the question of what kind of community Deleuze imagines after the fall of the law. Lastly, we will answer a criticism by Alexander Cooke, who claims that agrammatical resistance is easily incorporated by the law, and therefore becomes an impotent way of resisting it.

2. Bartleby, the Scrivener: A Story of Wall-Street

Bartleby, to begin, starts working as a scrivener in a lawyer's office: "At first, Bartleby did an extraordinary quantity of writing. As if long famishing for something to copy, he seemed to gorge himself on my documents."[3] After a few days the lawyer-narrator asks him to proofread a text, but "without moving from his privacy, Bartleby, in a singularly mild, firm voice replied, 'I would prefer not to.'"[4] He resists his boss's order, but not because he wants to rebel against his authority. He only *prefers* not to, but this says nothing about what he *wants*.[5] The lawyer-narrator is so disarmed by this reply that he doesn't even sanction it. He even starts to feel some kind of love for Bartleby and wants to help him. As time goes by, Bartleby starts to passively refuse more and more tasks until he ends up staring out of the office window, doing nothing. Even when he is fired, he prefers not to leave. The lawyer becomes so desperate that he moves his entire office to the other side of New York. Even then Bartleby doesn't leave, and he haunts the building until he is moved to 'the Tombs'.[6] Eventually Bartleby stops preferring to eat

3 BTS, 46.

4 BTS, 47.

5 BTS, 52.

6 BTS, 70.

and 'goes to sleep with the Kings and Counsellors.'[7] "Ah, Bartleby! Ah, humanity!"[8]

3. Resistance Against Paternal Community

If we want to agree with Deleuze that Bartleby announces a new democratic Messianism,[9] we first ought to know against what this strange Messiah reacts. What makes the world so wrong that we need a new Messiah? Deleuze's answer is that we need the dissolution of the paternal function to give birth to a new humankind.[10] Firstly, we will examine the wrongs of paternal community. What this new humankind should be is the topic of part 5.

Deleuze borrows heavily from Lacanian psychoanalysis to describe paternal community. Paternal Community is a way of living together that is founded on identification and mimetic rivalry.[11] When a subject (the son) identifies with an image or representation (the father), he must perform a certain effort to imitate and appropriate the image. This operation risks either falling into neurosis (when the subject cannot handle the image of the father) or narcissism (when the subject appropriates the image). In both cases, the relation between the son and the father is marked by 'mimetic rivalry', or 'aggressivity' in Lacanian psychoanalysis.[12] For Lacan, the image shows a kind of unity that cannot be achieved by the identifying subject, and that threatens the body with disintegra-

---

7 BTS, 73.

8 BTS, 74.

9 BOLF, 112.

10 BOLF, 108.

11 BOLF, 99.

12 BOLF, 99; J. Lacan, "Aggressivity in Psychoanalysis," in *Ecrits: A Selection* (London: Routledge, 1999), 8-29.

tion.[13] The body reacts with a latent aggressivity towards the image. A good example of this is the effect of seeing one's specular image in the mirror without knowing that one is viewing oneself.[14] This never leaves a good impression. Our natural response to our own image is one of repulsion, because it is a unity that haunts the chaos that is our real self.

Apart from the imaginary function as an image of identification, the father serves a second role in Lacanian theory. When Deleuze talks about "*une fonction paternelle*,"[15] he is quoting Lacan who uses the paternal function—the name-of-the-father and the symbolic father as synonyms.[16] The function of the father is to impose the law, and thereby give rise to desire in the subject. The father is the one who prohibits the *Dual Union* between the child and the mother by establishing the Oedipus complex and the fear of castration. The law shows itself first as a prohibition that is essentially linked to language. The name-of-the-father (*le nom-du-père*) is the no-of-the-father (*le non-du-père*).[17] Through barring direct contact with the mother, the child can only have access to her by identifying with the paternal function (with mimetic rivalry as a result) and by subjecting himself to the law of the father. Both Lacan and Deleuze use language as the paradigmatic example of the law. For Lacan, the law

---

13 Dylan Evans, "Aggressivity," in *An Introductory Dictionary of Lacanian Psychoanalysis* (London: Routledge, 1996), 6.

14 Freud comments on this experience in S. Freud (1999), "Das Unheimliche" in *Gesammelte Werke: Werke aus den Jahren 1917-1920*, pp. 262-263n1.

15 BOLF, 99.

16 Dylan Evans, "Father," in *An Introductory Dictionary of Lacanian Psychoanalysis* (London: Routledge, 1996), 62.

17 See, for example, the odd translation of his lectures in English, where the term 'No/Name of the Father' is used: Jacques Lacan, *The Ethics of Psychoanalysis* (London: Routledge, 2008).

imposes a social role or identity upon the child that pre-exists it, and it establishes language as a way of relating to the desired object within the paternal prohibition. As a result, desire is the lack of a lost object (*manque-à-être*) that one can never fill, for one needs to transgress the law to achieve the lost object, but this transgression eliminates the identity of the desiring subject.[18] Transgressing the law means transgressing the individual identity founded on the law and identification. *Le symbole est le meurtre de la Chose* in the sense that language blocks the way to objects and instead forces them into representations. Because of the law, the subject is doomed to eternally circle around the desired object without reaching it.

Deleuze agrees with Lacan's description of the link between language and the law, but comes to an opposite conclusion. According to Deleuze, from the standpoint of the law (in the short-story symbolized by the lawyer-narrator), language has two functions. (1) It suggests a system of references or assumptions that permit language to designate.[19] This means that language needs a system of rules whereby words are put in a certain order for them to be able to reach out to the world. For instance, if I want to talk about my dog sitting on the couch, then I need rules of syntax and semantics for my utterance to be meaningful. Just as in Lacan, this presupposes that the thing itself (*la Chose*) is substituted for its representation. (2) Language also presupposes a regulation of speech-

---

18 Jacques Lacan, *The Ego in Freud's Theory and in the Technique of Psychoanalysis* (Cambridge: Cambridge University Press, 1988), 223; Dylan Evans, "Signifying Chain," in *An Introductory Dictionary of Lacanian Psychoanalysis* (London: Routledge, 1996), 187-188; Lacan calls this experience of transgression '*jouissance*' (Jacques Lacan, *The Ethics of Psychoanalysis* (London: Routledge, 2008), p. 217).

19 BOLF, 95.

acts.[20] When one speaks, one is performing a social deed that has to be linked to a social role. I can't marry right now, because I am not in the social role of someone who is engaged to a woman and stands at the altar. Even if I say, "I do" after a friend says the same words as the priest does at a marriage, my speech-act will not consecrate the marriage, for neither I nor my friend are the appropriate persons for these speech-acts. I have to subject myself to these laws in order to become a subject, or, in other words, I have to become a particular within a system that has its own logic independent of me. Opposing Lacan, however, Deleuze does not conclude that the life of this particular is doomed to search an unreachable outside. Desire is not a lack, but a productive force.[21] The subject is always already outside language and the law, but to prove this Deleuze needs the figure of Bartleby.

4. Agrammatical Resistance

The first description Deleuze gives of Bartleby's "I would prefer not to" is that it is a formula. He does not, however, state clearly what a formula is. In a criticism of the article, Jacques Rancière starts with this topic.[22] He distinguishes it from the story (*l'histoire*) and the symbol (*le symbole*). A story is an intrigue where the meaning of the text coincides with the tale being told. A symbol, on the other hand, is a sign that allegorically designates a hid-

20 BOLF, 95.

21 Gilles Deleuze and Felix Guattari, *Anti-Oedipus* (London: Continuum, 2004), 5; Rudi Laermans, "Verlangen," in Ed Romein *et al.* (ed.), *Deleuze Compendium* (Amsterdam: Boom Uitgeverij, 2009), 240.

22 Jacques Rancière, "Deleuze, Bartleby et la Formule Littéraire," in *La Chair des Mots* (Paris: Editions Galilée, 1998), 179; We will not examine this criticism, because it deserves a study on its own. Rancière presupposes a lot of information about both Deleuze's text and his own philosophy.

den meaning. A formula is a performance in the sense that it is a material deed that fulfills the materiality of a text. By saying 'I would prefer not to" Bartleby performs a deed that is typical for literature as such. He performs a speech-act in such a way as to render the world of representations inoperative.[23]

Deleuze describes Bartleby's formula "I would prefer not to" secondly as an agrammaticality.[24] An agrammaticality is an utterance that turns the ordinary rules of grammar on its head without becoming nonsensical sound. It undermines the rules of language without consciously opposing them. For instance, when one wishes to declare their love for someone else, sometimes one is so nervous that instead of "I am in love with you," one says, for example, "You are with love in me". Instead of stuttering oneself, he has, as it were, made language itself stutter.[25] In the same way, Bartleby's formula ruptures the foundations of language. We have already seen that Deleuze describes representational language as a system of rules of regulating the reference of words and the interaction of speech-acts. The formula undermines both.[26] (1) Because of the incessant repetition of the formula words become meaningless and the connection to the outside world is cut off. Words or signifiers only have signifieds because they are taken up in a differential system that produces the link between signifiers and signifieds. When all words become indistinguishable, due to formulaic repetition, differences erode and the system falls on its knees. The result is a void within language, a zone of

---

23 Jacques Rancière, "Deleuze, Bartleby et la Formule Littéraire," in *La Chair des Mots* (Paris: Editions Galilée, 1998), 180.

24 BOLF, 89.

25 Gilles Deleuze, "Bégaya-t-il," in *Critique et Clinique* (Paris: Les Editions de Minuit, 1993), 135.

26 BOLF, 95.

indistinction where words become meaningless stains on a paper. (2)Bartleby also ceases to have a social role. He doesn't abide to his role as subordinate to his boss, the lawyer-narrator, but neither does he clearly oppose him in order to become a rebel. "I would prefer not to" is not a will to nothingness, but a rising nothingness of the will.[27] He neither accepts nor denies his social role, but instead prefers not to conform to it. His will is unimportant, because it can only relate to the law (as affirmation or negation), while Bartleby has left the realm of the law altogether. Bartleby is no longer a particular in the system, but a singularity (which will be explained later on).

We should, however, be careful in reading Deleuze's criticism of representational language through the formula of Bartleby. Representationalism was already criticized from a completely different angle. Some philosophers, like Usener or Cassirer, claimed that the origin of language was not the representation of signifieds through signifiers. They also talk about a language within language, but for them this is a mythic language. Myth is language where the signifier and the signified are identical. That Deleuze doesn't intend to speak about myth is clear from his reference to Odysseus.[28] He links Bartleby's claim of not being a particular to Odysseus saying to be no one (*oudeis*). Odysseus answered this to the cyclops Polyphemus, who asked Odysseus' name. Odysseus tricks Polyphemus exactly because the latter uses mythical language. When Polyphemus hears that he is talking to *Oudeis*, he really believes that he is talking to no one. Signifier and signified are inseparably linked. Odysseus is exactly the one who ruptures this link. Odysseus becomes no one– a man without references, by rupturing

27 BOLF, 92.

28 BOLF, 96.

the link between signifier and signified.[29] Bartleby's formula, just as Odyseus's, should thus be viewed as breaking the link between signifiers and signifieds in such a way as letting signifiers become autonomous forces without reference to the world outside. The signifier without signifieds becomes the pure *potentiality* of being able to mean anything and therefore *actually* they mean nothing. The name is reduced to *oudeis*.

Contrary to Lacan therefore, Bartleby shows the existence of an outside of the law and language. Deleuze claims that the formula pushes language to its limits "in order to find the Outside, silence or music".[30] Where for Lacan the outside of language and the law is an absence (*La Chose est aussi l' A-Chose*),[31] for Deleuze it is abundance.

The question then becomes what this outside is. The outside of the law, which doesn't need its judgment, is life itself: "*C'est la vie qui justifie, elle n'a pas besoin d'être justifié.*"[32] To understand this, we should examine the criticism against psychoanalysis that Deleuze develops in the paragraph of the just quoted passage.[33] Deleuze argues that psychoanalysis doesn't grant an outside to the law, because it is itself a representative of the law. The psychoanalyst is the one who judges every affect, dream or slip of the tongue of the patient. He or she gives and demands reasons for every action of the patient and thereby puts behavior under the rule of reason. This is reminis-

---

29 For a more thorough analysis, see Theodor W. Adorno and Max Horkheimer, *The Dialectic of Enlightenment* (London: Verso Books, 1997), 60-69.

30 BOFL, 94.

31 Jacques Lacan, *The Ethics of Psychoanalysis* (London: Routledge, 2008), 169.

32 BOFL, 104.

33 BOFL, 104-105.

cent of Foucault's genealogy of psychoanalysis.[34] The latter finds its origin in the practice of confession, where the sinner must submit his or herself in a relation of power in order to expose his life to the priest. The sinner must confess all deeds and particularly all the (unconscious) thoughts that accompanied them. The psychoanalyst is not the liberator of desire, because in truth "one should not think that desire is repressed, for the simple reason that the law is what constitutes both desire and the lack on which it is predicated."[35] In psychoanalysis reason and the law govern.[36] If Deleuze wants to liberate desire and life, he can't subject them to the law. Instead he must show that desire and life are not a lack of being (*manque-à-être*) emanating from the law, but productive forces outside the law. Life justifies itself and doesn't need justification from above.

Deleuze resolves the tension between life and the law by claiming that life is absolute potentiality.[37] Life under the law is determined by properties that block potentiality or territorialize life within a strict system. One's identity can, for instance, be determined by being a German, a white male, etc. These identifications are images that construct our more fluid bodies within socially manageable constraints, but they refer ultimately to the

34 Michel Foucault, *History of Sexuality: The Will to Knowledge* (London: Penguin Books, 1998), 58-73.

35 Michel Foucault, *History of Sexuality: The Will to Knowledge* (London: Penguin Books, 1998), 81.

36 Lacan seems to realize this problem, but doesn't give an adequate solution. He only claims that the psychoanalyst should approach the patient "in a discreet fraternity", but he doesn't develop what this attitude should be (see Jacques Lacan, "Aggressivity in Psychoanalysis," in *Ecrits: A Selection* (London: Routledge, 1999), 29).

37 BOFL, 109; This point is also stressed by Agamben (see: Giorgio Agamben, "Bartleby, or On Contingency," in *Potentialities* (Stanford: Stanford University Press, 1999), 254-255).

paternal function. We can only be particulars within a paternal community. When Bartleby says that he is not a particular, he shows another possibility.[38] Maybe we can be living beings without being determined within a legal system. Instead of a particularity, Bartleby is a singularity. The difference is that one as a particular is defined through the representational qualities one receives from the law. In order to become an individual subject, one must first be subjected to the law. Deleuze opposes to this view on subjectivity the idea of the *homo tantum*.[39] The grand utopias of the modern world (America and the Soviet-Union) were founded on the hope of the human having to be nothing more than human. No longer should one be defined by his or her nation or his or her class. The call for a *homo tantum* is a call for a nationless and classless society. Deleuze claims that this bare life is not an abstract substance without meanings, but the source or process of infinite meanings that can never be domesticated to a fixed identity. For instance, the migrant who arrived in the United States hoping to achieve 'the American dream', is nationless and classless, but not in the sense of being empty or experiencing a lack of identity. Instead they experience an abundance of multiple identities. They can become anything and anyone. The *homo tantum* is not a lack of being, but the absolute potentiality of becoming.

5. The Possibility of Fraternal Community

Opposed to paternal community, Bartleby is a Messiah of fraternal community. This is no longer based on identification, but on rhizomatic becoming: *"Ce n'est plus une*

38 BTS, 69.
39 BOFL, 110.

question de Mimésis, mais de devenir."[40] Deleuze reports three important shifts.[41] (1) The expressed form (*forme exprimée*) is substituted for the trait of expression (*trait d'expression*), which means that the representation of the father is abolished. Instead a multitude of expressions, such as Bartleby's formula, arise from a horizontal network of singularities. (2) The subject no longer hopelessly imitates an image, but identifies with an other by becoming indistinguishable from it. (3) The result is universal fraternity without a father. All singularities are related to one another without being linked to a transcendent law structuring the whole.

Here it becomes necessary to discuss a criticism leveled by Alexander Cooke in an article called "Resistance, Potentiality and the Law: Deleuze and Agamben on Bartleby".[42] His critique gives a good opportunity to delineate the exact contours of fraternal community. Cooke's claims that Deleuze (and Agamben) overlook a key passage in Melville's text that is symptomatic of agrammatical resistance:

> '*Prefer not,* eh?' gritted Nippers. 'I'd *prefer* him, if I were you, sir,' addressing me [the lawyer-narrator]. 'I'd *prefer* him, I'd give him preferences, the stubborn mule! What is it, sir, pray, that he *prefers* not to do now?' Bartleby moved not a limb. 'Mr. Nippers,' said I, 'I'd prefer that you would withdraw for the present.'[43]

---

40 BOFL, 100.

41 BOFL, 100-101.

42 Alexander Cooke, "Resistance, Potentiality and the Law: Deleuze and Agamben on Bartleby," in *Angelaki* 10, no. 3 (2005), 79-89 (henceforth RPL).

43 BTS, 58.

While Deleuze stresses the use of the word 'prefer' in only one sense, Melville uses it in three ways.[44] (1)Bartleby says "I would prefer not to" as a kind of passive resistance characterized as agrammatical resistance. (2)Nippers, one of the other copyists, uses it as a negation of resistance, and thus reinforces the transcendent law. (3)The lawyer-narrator subsequently uses it to exercise his authority as Nippers' boss. Deleuze risks undermining his thesis by not mentioning the second and third usage. If the logic of preference can be used to exercise paternal authority, then there is no use in claiming that agrammatical resistance actually works. It seems as if the law can easily incorporate Bartleby's resistance. Cooke links this to a criticism of Negri and Hardt.[45] They see Bartleby as a figure of absolute refusal. Although refusal is certainly the beginning of liberatory politics, it is not revolution in itself: "What we need is to create a new social body, which is a project that goes well beyond refusal. [...]. This project leads not toward the naked life of *homo tantum*, but toward *homohomo*, humanity squared, enriched by collective intelligence and love of the community."[46] Cooke forgets to mention collective intelligence and only talks about the image of love.[47] This is not, however, a big problem, since Hardt and Negri's notion of collective intelligence is to a large extent inspired by Deleuze. Collective intelligence, or the general intellect, is the knowledge produced by the multitude (an ensemble of singularities with a common absolute potentiality) in immaterial la-

44 RPL, 87.

45 RPL, 88; Antonio Negri and Michael Hardt, *Empire* (Cambridge: Harvard University Press, 2000), 203-204.

46 Antonio Negri and Michael Hardt, *Empire* (Cambridge: Harvard University Press, 2000), 204.

47 RPL, 88.

bor.[48] In contemporary post-fordist economy, workers no longer primarily produce material goods like cars, refrigerators or chairs. Instead the main products of labor are communication, ideas and affects. A hairdresser, for instance, doesn't simply produce hairstyles, but primarily a 'good feeling' for the client. A business manager doesn't produce goods, but PR and innovative ideas for their company. These immaterial goods can only be produced by a collective of workers that is not structured hierarchically, but horizontally. A brainstorm session, for example, works only when workers can speak freely and creatively and are not hindered by a boss that determines the outcome beforehand: "[People] need an expanding web of others with whom to communicate and collaborate; the boss is increasingly merely an obstacle to getting work done."[49] The important point, however, is Cooke's and Hardt and Negri's claim that the story of Bartleby and Deleuze's description of it lack an image of love.

We can complement Cooke's criticism with a radicalization of his claim that the law can easily incorporate agrammatical resistance. Is the dissolution of the father desirable? Psychoanalysis knows already since Freud that it is easy to murder the father and thereby establish a community of brothers. The problem is that this deterritorialized community would fall into chaos. Once the law is destroyed, the brothers start a *bellum omnium contra omnes*. They can only resolve the conflict by inventing an imagined father (the totem) to which they can give the authority of the law again. This is the story of the

---

48 For a more thorough analysis: see Antonio Negri, *Reflections on Empire* (Cambridge: Polity Press, 2008), 60-79.

49 Antonio Negri and Michael Hardt, *Commonwealth* (Cambridge: Harvard University Press, 2011), 353.

primal horde.[50] This means that Deleuze's *homo tantum* can only exist virtually. In actuality, as soon as the community of brothers would be realized it would annihilate itself from the inside out.

We can summarize Cooke's criticism as follows: (1a) Deleuze's agrammatical resistance can easily be incorporated in the realm of the law and (1b) according to Freud, it should even be avoided. (2) Deleuze's depiction of the fraternal community lacks an image of love to give something positive to it, something beyond mere naked refusal. We can elucidate Deleuze's theory of fraternal community by answering these critiques.

(1a) Deleuze knows very well that agrammatical resistance can be taken up in the functionings of the law. The confusion lies in the fact that Deleuze calls his own theory messianic, while this might evoke a notion of absolute salvation in the mind of the reader. Bartleby, as a Messiah, seems to be presented as the one who will solve all the world's problems and instigate a new era of humanity. This interpretation, however, should be avoided at all cost. If we read Deleuze's claims about the Messianic more carefully, we see that he opposes it to two other principles, namely salvation and charity.[51] Both are, as theological concepts, dependent on a transcendent God who dictates the law. In the case of salvation, an other (the Messiah) is a representative of that law and judges

---

50 Sigmund Freud, *Gesammelte Werke: Totem und Tabu* (Frankfurt am Main: Fischer Taschenbuch Verlag, 1999), 178-179.

51 BOLF, 112.

the lives of all men.[52] In the case of charity, one becomes oneself a representative of the law to love thy neighbour. Both salvation and charity fall into the trap of making individuals into particulars in a divine plan. God has already configured the ultimate structure (or law) of the world and humanity is either subjected to it through a Messianic coming or subjects itself to it through love for the neighbour.

What is new about the messianism Deleuze wants to discuss is that it is essentially democratic.[53] Democracy means that power, and power is distributed equally. This is a completely different image than salvation or charity, as the subject renounces power in order to give it to a transcendent God. Power in democracy doesn't disappear, but is only reconfigured. Deleuze borrows here from Foucault's analytics of power.[54] He makes a distinction between violence and force.[55] Violence is directed towards passive objects; things that are completely determined by the violence that oppresses it. These things are particulars within a pre-determined system against which they can undertake nothing, since they are deprived of agency. Force, on the other hand, is directed not toward objects, but toward other forces. Power is then a relation of forces. This means that power is marked by a kind of equality in the sense that both poles of a power relations are equally

---

52 This seems to be close to Derrida's notion of democracy to-come. The Messiah is an absent-present figure of salvation that comes from above. The Messiah transcends history, since the messiah are absolute alterity (see Jacques Derrida, *Specters of Marx* (London: Routledge, 1994)). For Deleuze, on the other hand, Messianic democracy is immanent and not a transcendent figure to-come. It is already here as an unrealized potentiality (namely absolute potentiality itself).

53 That is why he writes '*démocratique*' in cursive (see: BOLF, 112).

54 Michel Foucault, "Le Sujet et le Pouvoir," in *Dits et écrits IV* (Paris : Gallimard, 1994), 222-243.

55 Gilles Deleuze, *Foucault* (Paris : Les Editions de Minuit, 1986), 36.

forces, but they only differ in strength. Another consequence is that power can never be localized in a single individual or institution.[56] Every force presupposes a counter-force to which it relates. This means that all power relations are also relations of resistance. In democracy, no one can occupy the empty place of sovereignty, since all power comes at the cost of resistance in such a way that no one can transcend the interplay of forces to become the sole dominator of life.

(1b) Does this idea of power not confirm Freud's warning? Isn't this interplay of forces the anarchy of the *bellum omnium contra omnes* of the primal horde? As a careful reader of Foucault, Deleuze knows that viewing power as a relation of competing forces doesn't entail anarchy, but can in fact be very ordered. This order is called a diagram. A diagram is a cartography of forces.[57] It is a model by which power-relations are structured in such a way that a single example (for instance, the panopticon) becomes a paradigmatic example for the power-relations in other domains (schools, hospitals, factories, etc.) while remaining immanent to those power-relations. The panopticon, for example, was not developed as a thought experiment away from socio-political practice. It was a defined strategy within an already existing field of power-relations (the prison). The panopticon is then a way of organizing this multiplicity of forces in such a way that it orders them into a structured whole. This whole is not the system of the law, in which the particulars no longer have agency and can't therefore resist the diagram, but a community with several peripheral resistances (e.g. delinquents hiding from the panoptic gaze) and nodal points of power (the prison officer). These diagrams then

---

56 Gilles Deleuze, *Foucault* (Paris: Les Editions de Minuit, 1993), 33-34.

57 Gilles Deleuze, *Foucault* (Paris: Les Editions de Minuit, 1993), 42.

give rise to a particular kind of society, for instance disciplinary society.[58]

The sovereign and his laws can be one of those diagrams, but he is certainly not the only one. There is, however, a major difference between viewing the law as a system, or as a diagram. As a system its particulars lack agency and cannot, therefore, resist and overthrow it for another diagram. The system has no outside. The singularities of Deleuze's democracy however "are always ready to liberate themselves to accomplish themselves."[59] Singular life is always already the law's outside. The law as diagram presupposes the agency of the singularities that produce it. This comes close to what Agamben calls the free use of the law.[60] Both for Deleuze and Agamben, the law should not be abolished for anarchy to take over. Instead the law can remain, but rendered inoperative.[61] Instead of blocking the absolute potentiality of life with the law, the law is subordinated to potentiality, which means that singularities change the law as their immanent power-relations change:

> One day humanity will play with law as children play with disused objects, not in order to restore them to their canonical use but to free them from it for good. What is found after the law is not a more original and proper use value that precedes law, but a new use

---

58 Gilles Deleuze, *Foucault* (Paris: Les Editions de Minuit, 1993), 43.

59 BOLF, p. 112.

60 Giorgio Agamben, "Une Biopolitique Mineure," in *Vacarme* 10 (2000) 4-10, http://www.vacarme.org/article255.html [retrieved 09/05/2013].

61 'Inoperativity" is here the English translation of '*inoperosità*', which is again the translation of Blanchot's notion of '*désoeuvrement*'.

that is born only after it.[62]

After Bartleby's resistance to the law, it is not restored to something more original (for instance, a mythic law and language), but it becomes the object of an incessant play of forces. These forces harbor an absolute potentiality to reconfigure the ordered structure of the democratic community.

(2) Is this community without love? On first sight Cooke, Hardt and Negri seem to be right. Deleuze hardly mentions love in his article and if he does, it is in a negative sense. He opposes Christian love in the sense of charity, as is already explained, and he calls the fraternal community: "*la communauté des célibataires*".[63] Celibacy doesn't seem to be a paradigm for love, especially if he already eliminated pastoral love (charity). Is there then no positivity in Bartleby's resistance? Is it only absolute refusal?

I will in this article propose that love is the fundamental affect of resistance, as argued for by Negri and Hardt.[64] To turn rebellion into revolution we need love as the creative element in the negation of the law. Fraternal community, or in their terminology the multitude, is a multiplicity of singularities engaging with one another. A singular act of a subject (for instance, telling your boss that you would prefer not to) only makes sense when it is connected to other singularities. Love binds these singularities together, instead of them isolating themselves from each other and leaving the intersubjective

62 Giorgio Agamben, *The State of Exception* (Chicago: Chicago University Press, 2005), 64.

63 BOFL, 108.

64 Antonio Negri and Michael Hardt, *Empire* (Cambridge: Harvard University Press, 2000), 413.

domain.[65] The paradigm of this love, according to Negri and Hardt, is the joyous life of Saint Francis of Assisi.[66] Against the law and domination Francis posed the joy of being in common with sister moon and brother sun. This brother or sister-hood of being is fraternal community. Joy is a force that is rooted in whatever is enjoyed, which means that Francis's joyous life is entwined in being itself. Being, for Negri and Hardt, is the absolute potentiality, or virtuality (in Deleuze's vocabulary),[67] of the multiplicity of singularities from which all beings arise. This is more Heideggerian than it seems. Also for the later Heidegger being is an event (*Ereignis*) of a clearing (*Lichtung*) that discloses and encloses beings to a *Dasein*.[68] For instance, the world is always disclosed to me in a particular way. When I am in a bad mood, the world will be disclosed as a dark and unhappy place. This doesn't mean I will be depressed forever. Instead I can execute my projects in order to change the world according to my desires. These desires however are not self-decided upon, but are also the result of my being thrown into the world. Being is the play in which I, as a thrown being, encounter the world, disclosed in a particular way, and in which I can act upon that world in such a way as to change or transcend it.

Absolute potentiality, or virtuality, has a similar function in the vocabulary of Negri and Deleuze. It is also a

---

65 A. Negri and M. Hardt base their theory on love because they wish to avoid Hegelian recognition. In Hegel's political philosophy subjects become a community by recognizing each other as free and equal subjects. This process however is dialectical, while Negri and Hardt want an undialectical, rhizomatic community.

66 Antonio Negri and Michael Hardt, *Empire* (Cambridge: Harvard University Press, 2000), 413.

67 Antonio Negri and Michael Hardt, *Empire* (Cambridge: Harvard University Press, 2000), 356-359.

68 Martin Heidegger, "Letter on Humanism," in M. Heidegger, *Basic Writings* (London: Routledge, 1993), 159-160.

play of forces from which the particular manifestations of beings emanate in relation to other beings. Absolute potentiality is an event within beings from which every actual expression of those beings arise. There is, of course, one crucial difference between Heidegger and Deleuze/Negri. Heideggerian being transcends all beings, while absolute potentiality is an immanent force within every singular being.[69]

For instance, Bartleby is actually an office clerk, but he could be anything just like the migrant from our previous example searching for the American dream. By saying 'I would prefer not to' to the lawyer-narrator, Bartleby shows that he cannot be pinned down by the social identity of an office clerk. He is a singularity escaping the boundaries of the law. What he will actually become after escaping the law is the result of the free play of potentialities. For this free play to occur, he must be rooted in a multitude of other singularities. Otherwise the fraternal community is no more than an ensemble of unrelated individuals. Francis's joyous love for being (as absolute potentiality) is the paradigm for the common in fraternal community. A fraternal singularity loves another singularity not just as a particular actual being, but as a source of infinite possible beings.[70]

When Deleuze reiterates his distinction between violence and force in his article on Antonin Artaud, he connects it to the theme of love.[71] He writes about the dif-

---

69 We will not further investigate this point, since it would lead us away from our topic to an analysis of the role of immanence and transcendence in Deleuze.

70 In fact, this is exactly the point of Agamben's "Bartleby, or on contingency". See G. Agamben (1999), "Bartleby, or on contingency" in G. Agamben, *Potentialities*, p. 266.

71 Gilles Deleuze (1993), "Pour en Finir Avec le Jugement," in *Critiques et Cliniques* (Paris: Les Editions de Minuit, 1993), 158-169.

ference between *combat-contre* and *combat-entre*:[72] "*Combat-contre cherche à détruire ou à repousser une force* [...], *mais le combat-entre cherche au contraire à s'emparer d'une force pour la faire sienne.*"[73] This distinction is remarkable, because Deleuze gives the example of a love letter.[74] In such a letter, there can be combat-against the loved one in the sense that one wants to oppress contrary, carnivorous forces. The main strategy is however a combat within in the sense that the lover tries to seduce the forces of the beloved to join the forces of the lover.

Using this example we can introduce love as a theme in Deleuze's Messianic democracy. Love is the affect that forces us to strategically seduce each other to relate to each other. In this way, a singular life can love other singularities by rooting itself in the absolute potentiality of others. Our forces become so intertwined that we become a (fraternal) community of singularities. That is how falling in love and seducing the other transforms itself into love. When we fall in love, our forces combat to become a community in which the combat can be a combat-within instead of a combat-against (which would presuppose two separate communities). When this is accomplished the forces are so intertwined that even when the person composed of these forces changes, they remain interconnected. This doesn't however seem to solve the question whether Deleuze can't be more specific about how such a Messianic democracy should be structured. We know that fraternal community is the absolute potentiality of singularities engaging in power-relations structured in diagrams, but what diagrams are necessary for democ-

---

72 Ibid., 165-167.

73 Ibid., 165.

74 Ibid., 165.

racy? Or does Deleuze prefer not to answer this question? Love can't give such a diagram, because it is itself only a power-relation that should be inscribed in a diagram. Even if it could be a diagram, Deleuze's account remains too vague to provide some concrete political order.

The fact that Deleuze doesn't answer this question should itself be seen as a potential answer. If Deleuze knew or thought he could know the answer, he would have given it to us. The fact that he didn't, suggests that he didn't believe it to be his job to provide the blueprint for a new community. Again, we should see this as an alliance to Foucault. Foucault distinguishes between the universal intellectual and the specific intellectual.[75] The first is the intellectual that provides blueprints for an ideal society, since they can base their reasons on general and universal principles. The latter doesn't have universal principles, because one knows that all knowledge is interwoven with historically specific power-relations. One only provides a critical ontology of the present and thereby gives the subordinated in contemporary power-relations the means to resist. When historical balances shift, we don't need to reaffirm old principles of salvation, but we could "look for new weapons".[76] The philosopher does not tell people what to do, but instead provides them the means to decide for themselves. It is the people in a democratic society that should decide how this democracy works, not Deleuze. He can't risk becoming a father himself.

6. Conclusion

We now have a clear view of what Deleuze intended to

---

75 Rob Devos, *Macht en Verzet* (Kapellen : Pelckmans Uitgeverij, 2004), 74-88.

76 Gilles Deleuze, "Post-Scriptum sur les Societés de Contrôle," in *Pourparlers* (Paris: Les Editions de Minuit, 1990), 242.

say in "Bartleby, ou la formule". He describes Bartleby as a figure of resistance. Through the agrammaticality of the formula, Bartleby resists paternal community founded on the law. Agrammatical resistance shows life to be the outside of language and the law as absolute potentiality. This means that the law can never fully integrate life. Every time it tries to perform violence to life, it operates as a force calling for counter-forces in the form of resistance. When the paternal function is abolished, Bartleby shows the way to a Messianic democracy. Life is no longer subordinated to the law, but the latter becomes the object of the free play of potentiality: *"C'est la vie qui justifie, elle n'a pas besoin d'être justifiée."*[77]

Bibliography

Adorno, Theodor W., and Horkheimer, Max. *Dialectic of Enlightenment*. London: Verso Books, 1997.

Agamben, Giorgio. "Bartleby, or On Contingency." In *Potentialities*, 243-271. Edited by Giorgio Agamben. Stanford: Stanford University Press, 1999.

—. *State of Exception*. Chicago: Chicago University Press, 2005.

—. "Une Biopolitique Mineure." *Vacarme* 10 (2000): 4-10.

Cooke, Alexander. "Resistance, Potentiality and the Law: Deleuze and Agamben on Bartleby." *Angelaki* 10, no. 3 (2005): 78-89.

Deleuze, Gilles. *Critique et Clinique*. Paris: Les Editions de Minuit, 1993.

—. *Foucault*. Paris: Les Editions de Minuit, 1986.

—. "Post-Scriptum sur les Sociétés de Controle." In *Pourparlers*, 240-247. Edited by Gilles Deleuze. Paris: Les Editions de Minuit, 1990.

Deleuze, Gilles and Guattari, Felix. *Anti-Oedpius*. London: Continuum, 2004.

Derrida, Jacques. *Spectres of Marx*. London: Routledge, 1994.

Devos, Rob. *Macht en Verzet*. Kapellen: Pelckmans Uitgeverij, 2004.

Evans, Dylan. *An Introductory Dictionary of Lacanian Psychoanalysis*. London: Routledge, 1996.

Foucault, Michel. *History of Sexuality: The Will to Knowledge*.

---

77 BOFL, 104.

London: Penguin Books, 1998.

Foucault, Michel. "Le Sujet et le Pouvoir." In *Dits et* Écrits IV, 222-243. Edited by Michel Foucault. Paris: Gallimard, 1994.

Freud, Sigmund. "Das Unheimliche." In *Gesammelte Werke: Werke as den Jahren 1917-1920*, 227-269. Edited by Sigmund Freud. Frankfurt am Main: Fischer Taschenbuch Verlag, 1999.

Freud, Signmund. *Gesammelte Werke: Totem und Tabu*. Frankfurt am Main: Fischer Taschenbuch Verlag, 1999.

Heidegger, Martin. "Letter on Humanism." In *Basic Writings*, 141-181. Edited by Martin Heidegger. London: Routledge, 1993.

Kundera, Milan. *The Unbearable Lightness of Being*. New York: Harper Perennial Modern Classics, 2009.

Lacan, Jacques. "Aggressivity in Psychoanalysis." In *Ecrits: A Selection*, 8-29. Edited by Jacques Lacan. London: Routledge, 1999.

—. *The Ego in Freud's Theory and in the Technique of Psychoanalysis*. Cambridge: Cambridge University Press, 1988.

—. *The Ethics of Psychoanalysis*. London: Routledge, 2008.

Laermans, Rudi. "Verlangen." In *Deleuze Compendium*, 237-251. Edited by Ed Romein, Marc Schuilenburg, and Sjoerd van Tuinen. Amsterdam: Boom Uitgeverij, 2009.

Melville, Herman. "Bartleby, the Scrivener: A Story of Wall-Street." In *Great Short Works of Herman Melville*, 39-74. Edited by Herman Melville. New York: Harper Perennial Modern Classics, 2004.

Negri, Antonio. *Reflections on Empire*. Cambridge: Polity Press, 2008.

Negri, Antonio and Hardt, Michael. *Commonwealth*. Cambridge: Harvard University Press, 2011.

Negri, Antonio and Hardt, Michael. *Empire*. Cambridge: Harvard University Press, 2000.

Rancière, Jacques. "Deleuze, Bartleby ou la Formule." In *La Chair des Mots*, 179-203. Edited by Jacques Rancière. Paris: Editions Galilée, 1998.

Tim Christiaens (°1992) is a student at the Catholic University of Leuven in Belgium, where he is currently obtaining a Master's degrees in philosophy and comparative and international politics. He is writing his Master's thesis on the relation between sovereignty and biopower in the works of Michel Foucault and Giorgio Agamben. Tim's main research interests are within Continental political philosophy, especially French post-structuralism

(Foucault, Deleuze, Baudrillard), Italian (post-)Marxist thought (Agamben, Negri) and German critical theory (Adorno, Benjamin, Habermas).

The Nature of Oz
The Cultural Logic of Nature Documentaries and Prison Films

Jason Walsh
Case Western Reserve University,
Cleveland, USA

1. Introduction

On the surface, nature documentaries and prison films are two cultural forms very far-removed from one another. Nature documentaries are educational, informational, 'objective,' and for audiences of all ages. Prison films are narratives, intended to be entertainment, and targeted towards more mature audiences. It does not seem like there would be very much for these two genres to say to each other. However, when we consider how they operate in mass culture and how they construct the spaces they take place in, we find that nature documentaries, starting with Walt Disney and the founding of the genre and continuing to this day, have a disconcerting amount in common with prison films.

2. Walt Disney the Man

Walt Disney spent his formative years in the rural town of Marceline, Missouri. It was here that he developed "a special feeling toward animals that he would never lose."[1] Disney loved and was fascinated by animals for all of his life, and a conviction that other people felt similarly led him to produce the True-Life Adventure series: "nature documentaries that brought Walt's old narrative skills to natural events."[2] Starting with *Seal Island* in 1948, Disney, the man, helped to invent a narrative form that Disney, the company, along with others, would continue far into the future: "*Seal Island* would become the model not only for Disney documentaries but for nature documentaries generally."[3] According to Alex Wilson, "[t]he Disney studios popularized the genre of the wildlife movie in the early 1950s, and the influence of their work was felt in nature education for the following two decades."[4] Walt Disney's feelings towards animals heavily influenced the Disney company's nature documentaries, which in turn influenced the burgeoning genre.

Other aspects of Disney's personality found their way into his nature documentaries (as well as the rest of Disney's products), and provide a striking parallel to Jean Baudrillard's theory of the hyperreal (discussed below). Beginning with his earliest animations, Disney attempted to create an alternative world he could escape into, his own private utopia: "It had always been about control, about crafting a better reality than the one outside

---

1 Neal Gabler, *Walt Disney: The Triumph of the American Imagination* (Vintage, 2007), 11.

2 Ibid., 446.

3 Ibid.

4 Alexander Wilson, *The Culture of Nature: North American Landscape from Disney to the Exxon Valdez*, First Edition (Blackwell Pub, 1992), 118.

the studio."[5] This attitude led historian Jackson Lears to argue that "[t]he quintessential product of the [Disney] empire would not be fantasy, but simulated reality."[6] Neal Gabler thus argued that Walt Disney "altered American consciousness, for better or worse, so that his country-men would prefer wish fulfillment to reality, the faux to the authentic."[7] Gabler, however, is short of the mark, as Disney may certainly have played his part in this, it was part of a larger turn in culture.

3. Towards an Idea of Mass Culture

Before we can consider how cultural representations of nature and prison operate, we must have a conception of mass culture. Louis Althusser's classic essay "Ideology and Ideological State Apparatuses" provides a good start-ing point. Althusser introduces the notion of Ideological State Apparatuses (ISAs), which include, but are not lim-ited to, religious institutions, public education systems, and mass culture.[8] These distinct ISAs may operate in different ways, but ultimately "the ideology by which they function is always in fact unified, despite its diversity and its contradictions, *beneath the ruling ideology.*"[9] Nature documentaries and prison films, then, as products of mass culture, should reproduce ideologies "beneath the ruling ideology."

The next helpful concept in understanding the simi-larity between these two genres is Theodor Adorno and Max Horkheimer's idea of 'the culture industry.' Adorno

---

5 Gabler, *Walt Disney*, 479.

6 Ibid., 482.

7 Ibid., 632.

8 Louis Althusser, *Lenin and Philosophy, and Other Essays* (New York: Monthly Review Press, 2001), 96.

9 Ibid., 98.

and Horkheimer, writing a few decades before Althusser and long before Baudrillard, argued that "culture now impresses the same stamp on everything."[10] This is because "[u]nder monopoly all mass culture is identical, and the lines of its artificial framework begin to show through."[11] The similarity between nature documentaries and prison films is one of the places where these lines show through.

Examining the parallels between Althusser's ISAs and Adorno and Horkheimer's culture industry is a useful way to explicate an idea of mass culture. We can view the culture industry as an ISA, and consider the 'identical stamp' that the culture industry imprints upon all of its products to be the 'ruling ideology' that ISAs similarly leave on everything they (re)produce. Adorno and Horkheimer argue that, within the confines of post-World War II capitalism

> [e]veryone is guaranteed formal freedom. No one is officially responsible for what he thinks. Instead everyone is enclosed at an early age in a system of churches, clubs, professional associations, and other such concerns, which constitute the most sensitive instrument of social control.[12]

Althusser (consciously or not) elaborates on this, broadening Adorno and Horkheimer's concept of the culture industry to ISAs in general. Althusser argues that the reproduction of the conditions of production (including culture, values, morality, etc) are essential to the reproduction of a mode of production. Therefore, ISAs, like "churches, clubs, professional associations" or the culture

10 Theodor Adorno and Max Horkheimer, *Dialectic of Enlightenment* (NY: Continuum, 1989), 120.

11 Ibid., 121.

12 Ibid., 149.

industry, are integral to the reproduction of the mental state, "a constant reproduction of the same thing,"[13] which is in turn integral to the reproduction of the capitalist mode of production. In another parallel to Althusser, Adorno and Horkheimer remark that one of the features of the culture industry is "obedience to the social hierarchy."[14] Adorno and Horkheimer's culture industry, with its "obedience to the social hierarchy" and constant reproduction of the mental conditions of production, fits neatly into Althusser's theory as one example of an ideological state apparatus.

4. The Postmodern Turn

This theory of mass culture, as an ideological state apparatus that reproduces the ruling ideology of capitalism and helps reproduce the conditions necessary for the survival of the capitalist mode of production, is not quite enough, however. Adorno, Horkheimer, and Althusser were all writing in the 1960s or earlier, before or on the cusp of postmodernity (following David Harvey, we can take the end of Bretton Woods and the recession of 1973 as signal events of postmodernity and changes in the structure of capital).[15] In order to understand how nature documentaries and prison films function in postmodern culture, Baudrillard's theory of the hyperreal is necessary. It is a testament to Adorno and Horkheimer's analysis (as well as their writing), however, that their work presages Baudrillard in many senses and is more direct.

Baudrillard's theory of the hyperreal rests on his claim that the real no longer exists; we are left with only

13 Ibid., 134.

14 Ibid., 131.

15 Perry Anderson, *The Origins of Postmodernity* (New York and London: Verso, 1998), 78–79.

simulations of it. However, if the real no longer exists, we must have a new definition of simulation, or we are paradoxically simulating a real that does not exist. Thus, for Baudrillard, simulation is now "the generation by models of a real without origin or reality: a hyperreal. The territory no longer precedes the map, nor does it survive it. It is nevertheless the map that precedes the territory– precession of simulacra."[16] In Baudrillard's words, there is "[n]o more mirror of being and appearances, of the real and its concept."[17] Reality is now based upon simulations, which themselves do not have any grounding in a 'real.' Adorno and Horkheimer are writing in a different context, but their phrase "[t]he whole world is made to pass through the filter of the culture industry"[18] is apt here. Their description of post-World War II cinema gets very close to the hyperreal:

> The old experience of the movie-goer, who sees the world outside as an extension of the film he has just left (because the latter is intent upon reproducing the world of everyday perceptions), is now the producer's guideline. The more intensely and flawlessly his techniques duplicate empirical objects, the easier it is today for the illusion to prevail that the outside world is the straightforward continuation of that presented on screen.[19]

In an appropriately Marxist reversal, it is no longer

16 Jean Baudrillard, "Jean Baudrillard - Simulacra and Simulations - I. The Precession of Simulacra," accessed April 3, 2013, http://www.egs.edu/faculty/jean-baudrillard/articles/simulacra-and-simulations-i-the-precession-of-simulacra/.

17 Ibid.

18 Adorno and Horkheimer, *Dialectic of Enlightenment*, 126.

19 Ibid.

movies that approximate real life but real life that approximates the movies. Indeed, "[r]eal life is becoming indistinguishable from movies."[20] Baudrillard one-ups Adorno and Horkheimer by saying that the real has been destroyed. Real life and the movies are indistinguishable because real life no longer exists. Again, Adorno and Horkheimer explicate the consequences more clearly than Baudrillard: "Because of this ubiquity, the film star with whom one is meant to fall in love is from the outset a copy of himself. Every tenor voice comes to sound like a Caruso record, and the 'natural' faces of Texas girls are like the successful models by whom Hollywood has typecast them."[21] A Caruso record does not sound like your friend's tenor voice, nor does the actress look like your friend from Texas: your friends sound and look like the culture industry's products.

5. The Verite Experience as the Product of the Hyperreal Culture Industry

The loss of the real to the hyperreal has led a rise in what we can follow Baudrillard in calling the *verite experience*. Writing about the Loud family television experiment of the 1970s, Baudrillard says "In this 'verite' experience it is not a question of secrecy or perversion, but of a sort of frisson of the real, or of an aesthetics of the hyperreal, a frisson of vertiginous or phony exactitude, a frisson of simultaneous distancing and magnification, of distortion of scale, of an excessive transparency."[22] The verite experience promises access to a real that no longer exists, and

---

20 Ibid.

21 Ibid., 140.

22 Baudrillard, "Jean Baudrillard - Simulacra and Simulations - I. The Precession of Simulacra."

this is its appeal. This concept of the verite experience, as a product of the culture industry operating in the hyperreal, allows us to finally see the connection between nature documentaries and prison films.

What unites nature documentaries and prison films is that both construct spaces the average consumer does not have access to. The former provides access to a space we think we do not have access to because of the way 'nature' is constructed in culture, and the latter provides access to a space we do not *want* access to. Cultural constructions of nature and prison are prime examples of hyperreality; the simulations produced by the culture industry are the authentic, authoritative source of what nature and prison *are* and of what and how we think about them. Watching Disney's documentaries makes you a naturalist; watching all six seasons of HBO's *Oz* makes you an expert on prison life.

The 'nature' of nature documentaries is a "pure, unadulterated, authentic force that stands in contrast the artificial, compromised world of humans."[23] This raw, unadulterated nature is a space we can only access through simulations of it. Wilson argues that "[m]ost North Americans see wildlife on TV or at the movies before they see it 'live' in the form of the zoo, animal park, or campground."[24] Media representations offered by nature documentaries are experienced before 'real nature' ever is. In a natural progression from Adorno and Horkheimer's movie-goer, we now expect our experiences at the "zoo, animal park, or campground" to reflect what we have already 'learned' about nature from TV or movies. When watching a nature documentary, "animal performance in front of a camera is presented as animal

---

23 Mike Budd and Max H. Kirsch, eds., *Rethinking Disney: Private Control, Public Dimensions* (Wesleyan, 2005), 204.

24 Wilson, *The Culture of Nature*, 122.

behavior."[25] For Baudrillard, the paradox of the Loud family is that the audience is told "[t]hey lived as if [the camera crew] were not there. An absurd, paradoxical formula – neither true nor false: Utopian."[26] This is the paradox of the verite experience in general, and leads to what Baudrillard calls "simultaneous distancing and magnification." In the context of nature documentaries, "the closer the members of a film crew get with their cameras and paraphernalia, the further nature recedes from their experience, and ours."[27] Thus, "[n]ature in these movies is both impossibly close and impossibly distant, and perhaps that is our fascination with it."[28] We see the same effect of the verite experience operating in the Loud family and in nature documentaries. Performance is taken as behavior, because it is impossible to know whether it is performance or behavior; if we remove the cameras to check if everything stays the same, we lose the ability to check.

With a few caveats, much of the same applies to cultural representations of prison. The average consumer experiences prison on TV or in a movie before (if ever) experiencing a physical penitentiary. HBO's promotional materials for *Oz* invite us to "Spend Some Time Inside,"[29] emphasizing the (hyper)realism of their show. Just as nature documentaries instill an idea of nature as a pure, unadulterated other space, "[t]he prison as concept is an idea ingrained into the popular consciousness of what prison

---

25 Ibid., 123.

26 Baudrillard, "Jean Baudrillard - Simulacra and Simulations - I. The Precession of Simulacra."

27 Wilson, *The Culture of Nature*, 122.

28 Ibid., 125.

29 "Oz Poster," accessed April 5, 2013, http://ecx.images-amazon.com/images/I/51WOTHlesaL._SS500_.jpg.

might be."[30] As a consequence of hyperreality, "[t]he social and physical reality of prisons is constantly mystified and mythologized."[31] The prison is a hyperreal space obscured and hidden by simulations of it.

Curiously, it is mystified and mythologized in a way strikingly similar to Foucault's description of the Panoptic prison. (How fittingly hyperreal it would be if HBO based their cultural depiction of prison on a theoretical work instead of on a real prison.) Foucault claims that "the major effect of the Panopticon [is] to induce in the inmate a state of conscious and permanent visibility that assures the automatic functioning of power."[32] In *Oz*, there is a central control area where guards sit with all the inmates surrounding them in clear glass cells. Augustus Hill, the show's narrator, remarks that "everybody sees what everybody's doing."[33] Similarly, Foucault describes the Pantopicon as "[e]veryone locked up in his cage, everyone at his window, answering to his name and showing himself when asked."[34] One of the most frequently recurring scenes in *Oz* is roll call, in which all prisoners stand outside of their cell and answer, one by one, when their name is called out.

While slightly different because *Oz* is a dramatic narrative and not a documentary, the verite effect is still present. It operates in a slightly different context here: cultural representations of incarceration keep prison "distant, remote, and unknown, but at the same time,

---

30 Paul Wright, "The Cultural Commodification Of Prisons," *Social Justice* 27, no. 3 (Fall 2000): 15–21.

31 Ibid.

32 Michel Foucault, *Discipline & Punish: The Birth of the Prison*, 2nd Vintage ed (Vintage, 1995), 201.

33 Darnell Martin, "The Routine," *Oz* (HBO, n.d.).

34 Foucault, *Discipline & Punish*, 196.

nearby, an immediate threat of imaginable evil."[35] Baudrillard's simultaneous distancing and magnification is present in *Oz*. The "immediate threat of imaginable evil" is maintained through the character of Tobias Beecher, one of the central characters of the first season. He is a white, middle class lawyer (i.e. representative of HBO's target audience) who has been imprisoned for killing a child while drunk driving. But, at the same time, the prison in *Oz* is depicted as something distant: virtually no scenes take place outside of prison, and it is never made explicit what city or state the prison is in. The threat that 'this could be you' is always present while simultaneously maintaining the prison as something out of sight and out of mind.

6. Ideology Critique

If nature documentaries and prison films both operate as verite experiences, they also both reproduce similar ideologies. Writing about Disney's earliest nature documentaries from the 1950s and 60s, Wilson says that they draw on "a number of themes: friendships, animal instinct, predation and violence, natural disasters, and the idea of territory."[36] Sixty-some years later, similar ideologies are at work in Disneynature's production *Earth*. The animals featured live in an "increasingly dangerous new world" where they have to cope with the "harsh reality of life."[37] The film opens on a family of polar bears who are trying to deal with the ever receding sea. Throughout the documentary, global warming is a constant threat in the background, mentioned over and over. Just like HBO's

35 Wright, "The Cultural Commodification Of Prisons."

36 Wilson, *The Culture of Nature*, 117.

37 *Disneynature: Earth* (Walt Disney Studios Home Entertainment, 2009).

prison, Disney's nature is a dangerous place where everyone fends for themselves in order to survive.

The trope of the hunt is equally ever-present. In a phrase surprisingly reminiscent of the Pantopicon, *Earth* informs us that "where there are herds, there is always someone watching." We then get to watch as "a timeless ritual plays itself out: the drama of the hunter and the hunted."[38] In a tone of voice that suggests maybe we should return to it, we are told that "this is the circle of life that most of us in our urban lives have lost touch with."[39] Describing life in prison, Augustus Hill tells us that "the predators rise, take control, and make the rules."[40] In what could just as easily describe HBO's prison, *Earth* informs us that the African desert is "a land where only a few can survive. A special few."[41] And in what could just as easily describe *Oz's* sometimes-competing and sometimes-cooperating prison gangs, *Earth* tells us about how "elephants are forced to share the water with others. These are fragile alliances."[42] Competition for resources is natural; sharing and being sociable is not. John Berger, writing in a slightly different context, unifies these by arguing that "[t]his reduction of the animal, which has a theoretical as well as economic history, is part of the same process as that by which men have been reduced to isolated productive and consuming units."[43] Disney's nature documentaries and HBO's *Oz* reproduce an ideology of animal and man as competitive, individualistic creatures living in a world strictly governed by survival of the

38 Ibid.

39 Ibid.

40 Martin, "The Routine."

41 *Disneynature*.

42 Ibid.

43 John Berger, *About Looking*, 1st Vintage International ed (New York: Vintage International, 1991), 11.

fittest. This is present going all the way back to Disney's earliest nature films: Wilson describes how they served, in many ways, as "an appendage of the ideologies of the frontier and the free market, in which it's every 'man' for himself" and that they "[assured] us that aggression and the notion of private property have a natural origin."[44]

If *Earth* and *Oz* reproduce similar capitalistic ideologies of individualism and competition, they also both have consequently shunted visions for the future. Here the parallels between Disney's shallow conservationism and HBO's tepid gestures at prison reform speak for themselves. *Earth* and *Oz* are both fine examples of the Situationists' idea of recuperation, what Wright calls mass culture's ability to "co-opt, neutralize, and render powerless any challenges to the economic and political status quo."[45] Disney's nature documentaries and HBO's *Oz* both make reference to systemic problems and gestures towards solutions, but the narrative is always recuperated by the hegemonic discourse around these issues.

A Disney film about fishing "doesn't discuss the global economy that encourages industrial fishing, [but] it does succeed in conveying, on a visceral level, its character."[46] *Earth* constantly mentions global warming as a threat to animal life, but offers no analysis of its causes or ways to work against it. *Oz* makes motions towards acknowledging the systemic, root causes of mass incarceration, and then dismisses them out of hand. The narrator (a prisoner) mentions "the system that dumped us in here,"[47] but then continues to ridicule any attempts at reforming inmates because none of them want to be saved, reinforc-

---

44 Wilson, *The Culture of Nature*, 135.

45 Wright, "The Cultural Commodification Of Prisons."

46 Wilson, *The Culture of Nature*, 139.

47 Martin, "The Routine."

ing the idea that all prisoners truly belong in prison.

Wright is again thoroughly accurate when he says that "the popular culture reinforces the message that those in prison deserve to be there and those who aren't in prison, don't."[48] *Oz* reinforces this hegemonic notion in spades. Every time a new character (prisoner) is introduced, the first (and usually only) thing you learn about their background is why they are incarcerated. This is accompanied by a flashback to the (usually grisly) crime, which hammers home the point that those in prison deserve to be there. There is hardly ever any discussion of *why* the crime happened, just a brutal visual for the viewer to be shocked and outraged by. Tim McManus, one of the main characters in the prison administration, is an idealistic reformer committed to "a new approach to the prison problem"[49] who tries to fight against this notion and 'save' the inmates. However, at almost every corner McManus is shot down by the prison administration and portrayed as naive and unrealistic. Other officials do not take him or his suggestions seriously, and the prisoners almost uniformly disappoint his various theories of ways to 'reform' them. Dissent and reform are allowed to exist, as long as everyone recognizes them as the silly and futile projects they are.

In a passage that works just as well for the global warming of *Earth* or the mass incarceration of *Oz*, Wilson writes that in Disney's early nature films, "the industrialization of wild lands is inevitable; it's only a matter of managing the bears so they'll be able to survive it. Whether or not *we* will survive industrialization is a question never considered."[50] Global warming and mass incarcer-

---

48 Wright, "The Cultural Commodification Of Prisons."

49 Martin, "The Routine."

50 Wilson, *The Culture of Nature*, 143.

ation are inevitable; it's only a matter of managing ourselves and prisoners to ameliorate the situation a little; whether or not *we* will survive global warming or incarcerating huge portions of society is not a question up for consideration. *Earth* acknowledges global warming, and *Oz* acknowledges mass incarceration and in some cases structural issues around it, but both offer thoroughly recuperated narratives; neither offers any serious or legitimate critique of the issues at hand. Instead, "a solution to our problems is not a matter of structural change but simply a matter of time and Yankee ingenuity."[51] High-tech engineering of the atmosphere can solve global warming without any examination of systematic overproduction, overconsumption, or an economic system that requires infinite growth; mass incarceration will be solved by clever new techniques of making inmates get along, instead of trying to understand why the United States imprisons more of its population than any country in history.[52] *Oz* lets us know that mass incarceration is a problem without leading us to "question whether imprisoning millions of people is a wise use of public resources, to ask who benefits from mass imprisonment, or to see if alternatives to prison exist."[53]

7. Notes Towards A Conclusion

The similarities between Disney's nature documentaries, from the early ones Walt Disney himself was involved in to Disneynature's contemporary productions, and HBO's *Oz* run deep. Both genres use the verite experience to construct a hyperreal space, and these simulations have

---

51 Budd and Kirsch, *Rethinking Disney*, 218.

52 Wright, "The Cultural Commodification Of Prisons."

53 Ibid.

come to substitute for any kind of real. These simulations, as products of the culture industry, are ideologically subservient to capitalist ideologies of competition and individualism, as well as hegemonic notions about global warming and mass incarceration. Both genres acknowledge serious problems surrounding their subject matter, but the solutions they offer are weak and compromised by recuperation.

However, this does not mean hope is lost. We must simply continue to recognize that this is the function of mass culture in late capitalism, and look elsewhere for our politics. Instead of looking to Disney to lead the way towards any kind of environmental justice and feeling satisfied with ourselves for watching Disney complain about global warming, we need to recognize that any critique of global warming coming from within the confines of global capital is going to be toothless. Instead of considering ourselves knowledgeable and informed about mass incarceration or prison life because we watch *Oz*, or expecting HBO to recognize and critique the prison-industrial complex, "we must pose and answer the not-so-complex questions of whom the criminal justice system works for and benefits, how crime, criminals, and victims are defined, what alternatives to prison are available, and how they can be implemented"[54] ourselves. Until then, Berger, Baudrillard, and Foucault will continue to be frighteningly accurate:

> Between industrial capitalism, dependent on manufacture and factories, and financial capitalism, dependent on free-market speculation and front office traders, the incarceration area has changed . . . The prison is now as large as the planet and its allotted zones

---

54 Ibid.

can vary and can be termed worksite, refugee camp, shopping mall, periphery, ghetto, office block, *favela*, suburb. What is essential is that those incarcerated in these zones are fellow prisoners.[55]

Disneyland exists in order to hide that it is the 'real' country, all of 'real' America t h a t is Disneyland (a bit like prisons are there to hide that it is the social in its entirety, in its banal omnipresence, that is carceral).[56]

Is it surprising that prisons resemble factories, schools, barracks, hospitals, which all resemble prisons?[57]

Bibliography

Adorno, Theodor, and Max Horkheimer. *Dialectic of Enlightenment*. NY: Continuum, 1989.

Althusser, Louis. *Lenin and Philosophy, and Other Essays*. New York: Monthly Review Press, 2001.

Anderson, Perry. *The Origins of Postmodernity*. New York and London: Verso, 1998.

Baudrillard, Jean. "Jean Baudrillard - Simulacra and Simulations - I. The Precession of Simulacra." Accessed April 3, 2013. http://www.egs.edu/faculty/jean-baudrillard/articles/simulacra-and-simulations-i-the-precession-of-simulacra/.

Berger, John. *About Looking*. 1st Vintage International ed. New York: Vintage International, 1991. "Fellow Prisoners." *Guernica / A Magazine of Art & Politics*. Accessed April 6, 2013. http://www.guernicamag.com/features/john_berger_7_15_11/.

---

55 John Berger, "Fellow Prisoners," *Guernica / A Magazine of Art & Politics*, accessed April 6, 2013, http://www.guernicamag.com/features/john_berger_7_15_11/.

56 Baudrillard, "Jean Baudrillard - Simulacra and Simulations - I. The Precession of Simulacra."

57 Foucault, *Discipline & Punish*.

Budd, Mike, and Max H. Kirsch, eds. *Rethinking Disney: Private Control, Public Dimensions*. Wesleyan, 2005.

Disneynature: Earth. Walt Disney Studios Home Entertainment, 2009.

Foucault, Michel. *Discipline & Punish: The Birth of the Prison*. 2nd Vintage ed. Vintage, 1995.

Gabler, Neal. *Walt Disney: The Triumph of the American Imagination*. Vintage, 2007.

Martin, Darnell. "The Routine." *Oz*. HBO, n.d.

"Oz Poster." Accessed April 5, 2013. http://ecx.imagesamazon.com/images/I/51WOTHlesaL._SS500_.jpg.

Wilson, Alexander. *The Culture of Nature: North American Landscape from Disney to the Exxon Valdez*. First Edition. Blackwell Pub, 1992.

Wright, Paul. "The Cultural Commodification Of Prisons." *Social Justice* 27, no. 3 (Fall 2000): 15–21.

Jason Walsh is a junior in the Department of Philosophy at Case Western Reserve University in Cleveland, OH, US. His main academic interests are in the critical theory tradition of the Frankfurt School, the history of Marxist thought and 20th century continental philosophy more broadly, and labor history and political economy. Jason's main non-academic interests are in bicycles from the 1970s and being obsessive about music.

Rhythm as Logos in Native World-Ordering

Sierra Mills Druley
University of Oregon, Eugene, USA

In his book, *The Dance of Person and Place*, philosopher and scholar Thomas M. Norton-Smith defines a world-ordering process as one that creates patterns in sense experience through space and time. He posits two major world-ordering principals within the Native American worldview, relatedness and circularity. In this essay, I argue that rhythm and its role in Native life serves as the impetus for both of Norton-Smith's world-ordering principals. I will show how rhythm, as presented initially by Lakota philosopher Robert Bunge, orders not only time but space as well and so can be understood as the logos that underpins the world-ordering principals of relatedness and circularity.

The indigenous peoples of North America had, and continue to have, many diverse cultures that emerged in response to varied social and ecological contexts. For the purposes of this essay I will speak of a "Native" worldview, but it is important to note that this worldview is a construct based on generalities made about a collection of distinct and autonomous nations. These generalities will be just as flawed and circumspect as those made about "European" or "Asian" cultures, but they do serve to illustrate some of the common themes in American Indian philosophy. The authors that I draw from write about particular tribes but they also address American Indian thought in general. What we find to be important, here, are the common philosophical and cultural threads between many tribes that, when taken together, constitute what we will call the "Native" worldview.

Part I: Norton-Smith and World-Ordering Principals

Thomas M. Norton-Smith introduces world-ordering principals as part of the larger process of world-organizing, which includes construction, deconstruction, weighting and ordering. Together, these processes are the mechanisms for world-creation through which cultures develop a functional understanding of how the world works, and their place within it. For the purposes of this study we will focus specifically on the process of ordering: the sorting of spatial and temporal sensory data so as to create patterns in the world that make it livable and intelligible for human beings. Norton-Smith proposes two world-ordering principals that he sees to be fundamental to a Native American worldview: relatedness and circularity.

The world-ordering principal of relatedness is illustrated in a phrase familiar to many American Indian tribes, "We are all relatives." This statement does not apply simply to the members of one's family, or to all of humanity. Rather, it implies that all living things—all of the elements and organisms on Earth—are inextricably woven together, related, as a family is. In this view, finding new information about the world involves seeking new patterns of relatedness within it. Instead of investigating the nature of a thing itself, a native person, Norton-Smith claims, would look for the connections that thing has with the others that surround it, thereby gaining some functional knowledge about how that thing operates in the world.

The statement "we are all relatives" implies reverence for the world that encompasses us. Norton-Smith writes, "In the Native world version, everything is related and we are all relatives, so all entities and beings are interconnected, valuable by virtue of those interconnections, and due respect."[1] Here we see that the indigenous world view that Norton-Smith describes is a fundamentally ethical one—a perspective wherein all things have intrinsic worth because of their relatedness to each-other and to the whole. So, an investigation must respect the relatedness of things by considering the impact that investigation has on other members of the human and non-human world. In this view, when we seek to gain information about the nature of things, we must do so carefully and thoughtfully—never imagining that we are detached, objective observers, but remembering that we are in fact deeply embedded in the world of experience, and accountable to it.

The second world-ordering principal that Norton-Smith gives us is circularity; while creating patterns of relatedness in sense experience, the Native worldview is one that generates circular patterns as well. Norton-Smith writes, "...Hunter-gatherer societies had to ob-

1 Thomas M. Norton-Smith, *The Dance of Person and Place: One Interpretation of American Indian Philosophy* (Albany: State University of New York, 2010), 59.

serve, create, and operate in accordance with seasonal patterns, with cyclical patterns imposed on temporal experiences—the ripening of berries in spring, late summer corn harvests, autumn migrations, and winter hunts—in order to survive. But such seasonal circular orderings are also spatial orderings—harvests and hunts are events in both time and space."[2] Here, we see that in the circular ordering of experience, spatial and temporal spheres coincide. For Native peoples, the natural cycles that order life have time frames and locations (even in July, you won't find strawberries at the top of Mt. Hood). Spatio-temporal circular patterns diffuse through many areas of native life—as Norton-Smith describes, tribes like the Lakota associate seasonal changes with the cardinal directions, merging the categories of time and space within one circular context with a distinct tribal center. So, the indigenous concept of circularity is one that extends through time and space to bring coherence to sensory phenomena.

There is something that underpins the two world-ordering principals that Norton-Smith gives us—a driving force that animates and solidifies them. If, indeed, we are dealing with a worldview wherein relatedness and circularity order sensory experience, then rhythm and its role in native life can serve as a functional logos for understanding these two principals--rhythm can demonstrate how these ordering processes shape the Native worldview. For an initial account of rhythm in indigenous life, we will look at the work of Lakota scholar Robert Bunge in his book, *An American Urphilosophie*.

---

2 Thomas M. Norton-Smith, *The Dance of Person and Place: One Interpretation of American Indian Philosophy* (Albany: State University of New York, 2010), 125.

Part II: Rhythm in Time and Space

Robert Bunge explicates a "Sioux Cosmology and Cosmonogy" that involves a view of humanity as a single participant in a multi-faceted and animate natural world. In it, he includes a description of rhythm as an ordering mechanism for temporal experience, and a grounding force in Native life. He writes that rhythm, for the Lakota, reflects "the 'pulse' or 'heartbeat' of all that is."[3] Since Native people view themselves as part of a living biotic world, the beat of the drum can be seen as a connection to the pulse that animates the entire universe. Bunge writes that "Time and rhythm are inexorably bound together" in the Native worldview, and describes how the pattern of the seasons and the cycles of the moon and sun are reflected in the rhythms of Lakota music.[4] In this way, rhythm connects Lakota people to the larger "natural" order of time in the universe—it connects them temporally to the world around them.

An implication of this understanding of rhythm that Bunge leaves out, and which I find essential, is the role of rhythm in ordering spatial experience. If rhythm, as Bunge claims, orients the Lakota people to the living world around them, then it has spatial qualities as well as temporal ones. And certainly, as we have seen through Norton-Smith, the categories may not be clearly parsed. So, though rhythm occurs in time, one beat following the previous one, it serves a spatial function by placing the Lakota in an outward-looking position to the whole of the pulsing world. A Lakota person listening and moving to rhythm, Bunge writes, is akin to "a kitten huddled

---

3 Robert Bunge, *An American Urphilosophie: An American Philosophy, BP (before Pragmatism)* (Lanham, MD: University of America, 1984), 53.

4 Ibid.

close to the breast of its mother."[5] Just as a child is part of (and comes from) its mother, the Lakota emerge as part of the animate universe through rhythm.

In his Sioux cosmology, Bunge describes how humans, and indeed all life, are participants in creation. The making of the world, for the Lakota, is a continuous process wherein all of the creatures of the Earth must participate in an active and continuous process that maintains the balance and rightness of creation. Bunge writes, "In a very real sense the universe of the tribe was personally upheld by the participation of every member in recreating and sustaining [the] universe."[6] Rhythm, here, can be seen as one such participatory process wherein humanity helps sustain the healthy heartbeat of the world. This notion accounts for the perceived "monotony" of Native drum beats, as Bunge puts it, "If it is even, regular, and monotonous, as the healthy pulse of a living organism should be, then the drum in rhythm with this pulse helps maintain this healthy state."[7] So, we see that Native drumming, insofar as it regulates and reinforces the people's relationship to the breathing biosphere, can be seen as a kind of care for or maintenance of the universe. In this way, rhythm solidifies the place of Native people as a demonstrative participant in the greater spatial universe to which they belong.

So, rhythm in the Lakota tradition represents an ontology ultimately rooted in a kind of fractal logic. Which is to say, just as the form of a fractal pattern is mirrored in the form of one of its parts (picture broccoli, where the larger "tree" is made of many tiny "trees"), the shape and pattern of Lakota rhythms mirror the heartbeat of the

5 Ibid., 54.

6 Ibid., 53.

7 Ibid., 54.

whole living world. Put differently, the people's drum beat represents one musical line that is ultimately the same, though smaller and less complicated, as the greater melody of the universe itself. This process orients the Lakota in space—it places them as an interior part of a surrounding whole, a whole that is reflective of each of its parts. Thus, the fractal relationship between Native rhythm and the rhythm of the biosphere underpins a Native cosmology. As the early twentieth Century anthropologist Alice Fletcher writes, "the natives of America thought of the cosmos as a unit that was throbbing with the same life-force of which they were conscious within themselves."[8] This "life-force" operates in the same way on the level of the whole as it does in Native drum rhythms on the level of a part. This is how, as Bunge writes, that through rhythm humans can access a "feeling of harmony or of moving in accord with the universe and, conversely, feeling the universe move within oneself."[9]

So, we can see that Rhythm facilitates a reflective connectivity between part and whole that constitutes a spatial ordering in the Native worldview that Bunge presents. And, as we established before, it also serves a temporal ordering function through the biological patterns of native life. From this point, we can begin to understand how rhythm can serve as an impetus for and connection between Norton-Smith's world-ordering principals, relatedness and circularity.

8 Alice C. Fletcher, *Indian Games and Dances with Native Songs: Arranged from American Indian Ceremonials and Sports* (Lincoln: University of Nebraska, 1994), 1.

9 Robert Bunge, *An American Urphilosophie: An American Philosophy, BP (before Pragmatism)* (Lanham, MD: University of America, 1984), 54.

Part III: Rhythm as the logos in Relatedness and Circularity

The first of Thomas M. Norton-Smith's Native world-ordering principals, relatedness, places human beings in intimate connection to the world around them. But relatedness by its nature also implies a kind of separation. If two entities are said to be related, they must in fact be distinct from each-other in some way. For example, if object A and object B have a relationship, C, then A and B cannot be the same—they are related to each-other through C, which connects them as it holds them apart. A relationship, then, is something that occurs between distinct entities. We can see now how this is a rhythmic principal; each note in a musical line is related to the next, and it is the spaces or pauses between beats that serve as the connective tissue. A breath between notes sets them in relation to each-other and helps shape the form of the musical whole. So, as much as beats in a sequence are related, they are also set apart by a pause or breath. This creates a tension between beats that pushes and pulls at the same time, initiating a dynamic relationship--rhythm.

In describing his principal of relatedness, Norton-Smith claims that our relationship to other beings in the sensorial world requires respect and reverence for the rest of the universe. Because our actions have implications for the entities we are connected to, we must consider those implications during our investigations into the world. Relatedness, for Norton-Smith, is the source of our desire to know and care for the world. As an interplay between connection and separation, between sound and pregnant silence, rhythm can help us understand the desirous nature of relatedness. We have established that rhythm is a force that lives in the anticipatory spaces between beats, as much as in the beats themselves. This necessary and incommensurable tension between the beats of a melody form a rhythm that is always seeking to consummate the relationship between notes, just as we seek to consummate the relationship between ourselves and the world. To illustrate this concept, we can take Bunge's example of the kitten and her mother; the kitten wishes to be close to her mother, but she can never be close enough so as to become one with her mother and so the connection remains perpetually incomplete. As rhythm brings us closer to the greater heartbeat of the world, it also reminds us that we are distinct from it as the part is distinct from the whole. It is our desire to be closer than we can ever really be to the world that drives the need to find ourselves within it, and to find the world within ourselves. It is the resounding gap between notes, and between ourselves and the elusive other, that shapes the rhythm of our unrequited love for the world.

Finally, the world-ordering principal of relatedness implies that in seeking knowledge about the world, we will look for patterns that connect things to each-other instead of properties of the things themselves. The advantage of this investigative strategy can be demonstrated through rhythm: in a rhythmic line or a melody, it is the relationship of the beats and notes to each-other that gives the line its meaning and tone. A single note, taken out of the context of its melody, is relatively meaningless and uninformative. The beats only mean something as part of the phrase. Similarly, a sea otter taken out of its habitat and studied in a lab will not demonstrate its role as a keystone species. The animal must be considered in the context of its complex marine ecosystem before its essential role in that ecosystem can be understood.

Norton-Smith's second world-ordering principal, circularity, posits that the Native world is organized by natural cyclical patterns—the turn of the seasons, the phases of the moon, animal migrations, and so on. These natural patterns provide the framework for circularity as a temporal ordering mechanism. We can see the temporal role of circularity at play in native drum rhythms: these rhythms contain repetitious phrases that move through time like the steady heartbeat of a healthy organism. As a phrase is completed, it circles back on itself, creating a rhythmic spiral that echoes the cyclical patterns of the natural world. But unlike the seasons that change throughout the year, or the monthly cycles of the moon, the rhythm of drumming happens in the present—in a tangible, concentrated time frame in which it is easy to decipher patterns of repetition. Rhythm, then, provides the initial context from which other cyclical patters in the world can be understood. The beat of the drum can serve as a perspective on time that situates Native peoples within a universe of natural refrains.

Circularity also functions as a spatial ordering principal in the Native worldview that Norton-Smith illustrates. It serves to orient phenomena in the world around spatial centers from which radiate spheres of meaning. These centers are points of spiritual and practical significance that serve to orient Native people within their life-world. Norton-Smith writes, "almost all tribal religions have a sacred place or geographic feature at its center—a mountain, plateau, or river among them. This religious center—this sacred place--helps the people to locate themselves with respect to their lands, the cardinal directions, and other non-human relations."[10] Rhythm, as Robert Bunge describes it, provides a centering or grounding force in Native life that pulls people toward such a center. He writes, "As long as the drum beats and singers sing...

---

10 Thomas M. Norton-Smith, *The Dance of Person and Place: One Interpretation of American Indian Philosophy* (Albany: State University of New York, 2010), 121.

conditions cannot become truly intolerable because men are, at that time, at the source of Being Itself."[11] Here, we can see that rhythm orients people toward the ultimate center of the "hoop of the world," as it is commonly described in Native America. Insofar as rhythm connects us to the pulse of the animate biosphere, it focuses our physical attention toward the source of life from which meaning emerges in the world. It places us in a spatial position with the living world—as a part within its whole. In this way, rhythm orients spatial, as well as temporal phenomena through circularity. Spatial, because it serves as motion toward a spiritual center that is located in the context of the land, and temporal because it constructs a basis from which to understand the passage of time through the natural cycles.

Rhythm, as we have applied it here, can be seen as a revelatory, or magical entity. It helps produce tangible versions of systems and patterns in the world that are unseen. It is an ontological tool that helps us know the nature of things, a kind of learning that is not explicit, literate, or visual, but visceral and real. Rhythm is a didactic demonstration of humanity's circular intertwining with the world, and, as such, serves as the fundamental ordering principal—the functional logos—on the basis of which we can understand the principals of relatedness and circularity. Rhythm, in the Native worldview, provides a subtle scaffolding for the flow of sensory experience—a temporal and spatial structure that places humanity in nuanced communion with the whole of the pulsing world.

---

11 Robert Bunge, *An American Urphilosophie: An American Philosophy, BP (Before Pragmatism)* (Lanham, MD: University of America, 1984), 54.

Bibliography

Bunge, Robert. An American Urphilosophie: An American Philosophy, BP (before Pragmatism). Lanham, MD: University of America, 1984.

Fletcher, Alice C. *Indian Games and Dances with Native Songs: Arranged from American Indian Ceremonials and Sports.* Lincoln: University of Nebraska, 1994.

Norton-Smith, Thomas M. *The Dance of Person and Place: One Interpretation of American Indian Philosophy.* Albany· State University of New York, 2010.

Sierra Mills Druley is a senior undergraduate in environmental studies and philosophy at the University of Oregon. She is currently writing an honors thesis focusing on phenomenology, ethics, and the design of built space. Sierra's additional areas of study include music performance, dance, and community development.

A Rejection of the Metacoherence Requirement

Ryan Scheuring
Chapman University, Orange, USA

In recent years some authors have argued that it is epistemically paradoxical for one to hold certain forms of belief while denying having knowledge that the belief is true. Supporters of this idea may hold something similar to the Metacoherence Requirement (MR): "Categorically believing that P commits one, on reflection, to the view that one knows that P."[1] On this view, if we have a categorical belief that "it is raining," reflect on it and are rational, then we must commit to the view that we know that it is raining. I hold this view to be mistaken, and in this paper I will argue that it is in fact epistemically rational or reasonable to sometimes hold a categorical belief that P without committing to have knowledge that P. This is due to the fact that asserting[2] that one has a categorical

---

1 Michael Huemer, "The Puzzle of Metacoherence," *Philosophy and Phenomenological Research* 82, no. 1 (2011): 1.

2 Assertion is, for my use, defined as a speech act in which a proposition is stated.

belief that P is inherently and categorically different than asserting P outright.

To state the categorical belief—P, is to make a claim about one's mental state. However, asserting P—or claiming that P is true—is to make a claim about an external reality. The two claims are about two categorically different things, and this difference explains why we can be epistemically rational in having a belief that P without having the additional claim to know that P.

I plan to advance an argument for *MR* and show why I believe it fails, lay out my reasons as to why I reject metacoherence as a requirement, and then finally answer some possible objections and explore the implications of my view. In short, I would like this paper to show that the Metacoherence Requirement is in fact not an epistemic requirement, and to produce a positive account of why we are sometimes epistemically reasonable in being meta-incoherent.

1. Huemer's Metacoherence Requirement

The Metacoherence Requirement argument I will be referring to is the one presented by Michael Huemer in his "The Puzzle of Metacoherence." Metacoherence is, according to Huemer, "...an epistemically desirable relationship between beliefs and metabeliefs" (1). In order to be epistemically rational, any categorical belief that P must be accompanied by a claim to know that P. Huemer outlines his reasoning:[3]

Suppose you have a categorical belief say, that

---

3 It is worth noting that Huemer does not spend a lot of time arguing for the Metacoherence Requirement. He offers these reasons appealing to the Moore-paradox, and simply asks the reader to assume MR is a plausible norm. He spends the majority of his paper attempting to explain MR.

it is raining. And suppose that you come to reflect explicitly on whether your belief constitutes knowledge. What conclusion might you come to? You must either conclude that you know that it is raining, or withhold judgement about whether you know this, or conclude that you do not know it.

If you conclude that you do not know it, then it seems that there will be a kind of tension between your first-order belief that it is raining, and your second-order belief about that first-order belief. If you hold on to your first-order belief while simultaneously denying that it constitutes knowledge, then, I think, you are guilty of some sort of irrationality. This is suggested by the fact that, were you to express your attitudes in words, you would utter a Moore-paradoxical sentence along the lines of 'It is raining, but I don't know whether it is raining.'[4]

This line of argument leads Huemer to suggest the Metacoherence Requirement (MR): "Categorically believing that P commits one, on reflection, to the view that one knows that P" (2). If MR is in fact a requirement, we would expect it to apply to all categorical beliefs (otherwise it wouldn't be a requirement). Further, in this paper, I would like to argue that this is not the case, and therefore the Metacoherence Requirement is not a requirement.

There are some definitional problems that are worth noting as well. I suspect Huemer of tweaking definitions to suit his argument, even though these changes shift

---

4 Huemer, "The Puzzle of Metacoherence," 1.

his view away from our everyday use of the term *belief.* Notice that MR only applies to a certain kind of belief: categorical belief. Huemer describes categorical belief as:

> a strong form of belief, to be contrasted with tentative or qualified belief. In particular, I assume that there is a species of belief of which two things are true: first, that it is the attitude normally expressed by assertion; second that it is the doxastic attitude required for knowledge.[5]

He also adds that he does not assume that categorical belief needs to be 100% certain. Categorical belief, then, is a narrow concept. For example, how might we describe a belief that is both not 100% and not tentative? Would we ascribe "tentative" to a belief with a credence less than 90% so that categorical belief would be 91%-99%? Any cut-off line for "tentative" that isn't certainty or 100% seems like it would have to be arbitrarily drawn.

Huemer then decides to refer to this narrow concept of "categorical belief" as simply "belief" for reasons that seem surreptitious and misleading (why not just call it Categorical belief? Or *CB,* if he wants to be terse?). The paper is misleading in that, while the impression is it has widespread implications for belief, the reality is that it only applies to a narrowly defined type of belief—one that is assumed by the author. We can see that even if Huemer is completely successful in his argument, the conclusion is a small one.

I would like also to call into question his claim that categorical belief is the "doxastic attitude required for knowledge."[6] Here, Huemer appears to constrict the re-

---

5 Ibid., 2.

6 Huemer, "The Puzzle of Metacoherence," 2.

quirements for knowledge as there are cases of what we would call *knowledge without any belief.* Let us take the case of blindsight,[7] wherein patients claim to be completely blind—this, despite access to visual stimuli which appears unconsciously—believing fully the proposition that they are blind. When asked whether they would participate in a test to assess their ability to decide whether a stick presented in front of them is vertical or horizontal, they are initially hesitant (after all—they believe they are blind!). Typically after some persuasion, the experimenter convinces the blind-seer to humor him or her. In these studies, the blind-seeing person does remarkably well in discerning the position of the stick, which is much better than the 50% accuracy we would expect to see as a result of simple guessing.[8] We can assume then that the patients were not guessing, and instead they had knowledge of the stick's orientation. The patients seemed to know the stick's position without believing that they could know it. The alternative would be that they are guessing remarkably well—or that the blind-seers are mistaken or lying about their blindness.

Nonetheless, some will claim that these blind-seers, without internal justification, don't have knowledge of the orientation of the stick—so be it, as my argument doesn't hinge on this idea.[9] Huemer seems to be mistaken in his description of categorical belief as a doxastic

7 Blindsight is the ability of people who are cortically blind due to lesions in their striate cortex, also known as primary visual cortex, to respond to visual stimuli that they do not consciously see, and therefore do not believe to see.

8 Laura Chivers, "Blindsight and Consciousness." *Serendip Studio,* Published 1/3/2008. Accessed on 12/2/2013. http://serendip.brynmawr.edu/exchange/node/1676.

9 For a more persuasive example of knowledge without belief, see page 14.

attitude required for knowledge. If categorical belief is, as I believe, not required for knowledge, then likewise a commitment to knowledge is not so clearly entailed by categorical belief.

Some might say that the doxastic attitude involved when asserting a belief like "it is raining" is the same attitude that involves an outright assertion of the proposition "it is raining." While I agree that any belief comes with some level of conviction, I don't think that the conviction always necessitates an outright assertion of the proposition. If someone has the belief "it is raining" they probably do have some sort, or amount of, conviction to the truth of that proposition. It would be strange to say, "I believe that it is raining, but I really don't have any conviction either way." However, I don't see how this conviction would have to be strong enough to commit the believer to an assertion (and therefore a claim to knowledge) in every case. Hence, there is nothing epistemically wrong with saying, "I believe that it is raining, but I don't know whether it's raining."

I suppose that anyone who holds that any categorical belief in P always necessitates an attitude that involves outright assertion that P won't be convinced by my argument, though I cannot imagine any reasons to feel this way. In fact, Huemer admits that categorical belief is only "normally" expressed by assertion—but that discussion will have to wait for further development.[10]

2. Inherent Difference in Belief in P and Asserting that P

The definitional contours of categorical belief do seem to be designed with Huemer's argument in mind—when we

---

10 Huemer, "The Puzzle of Metacoherence," 2.

do claim to have knowledge, it is an attitude normally expressed by assertion, and that, obviously, it is a doxastic attitude required for knowledge. Though there is a strong connection between claiming to know that P, and also believing that P—belief that P does not always rationally commit one to the view that one knows that P—even within his own definition of categorical belief. Let's look at Huemer's argument again:

> Suppose you have a belief say, the belief that it is raining. And suppose that you come to reflect explicitly on whether your belief constitutes knowledge. What conclusion might you come to? You must either conclude that you know that it is raining, or withhold judgement about whether you know this, or conclude that you do not know it.[11]

Huemer then supposes that if we conclude that denying or even withholding the claim that you know it, holds the believer guilty of "some sort of irrationality."[12] He offers support for this claim: "were you to express your attitudes in words, you would utter a Moore-paradoxical sentence similar to 'It is raining, but I don't know whether it is raining.'"[13] I agree that this sentence is contradictory; however, the analogy is imprecise. Huemer simply assumes that the statement, "I believe it is raining," is equivalent to "it is raining," which is simply false. When one says, "it is raining" it does in fact seem that they are making a claim about an external reality.[14] For that rea-

---

11 Huemer, "The Puzzle of Metacoherence," 1.

12 Huemer, "The Puzzle of Metacoherence," 1.

13 Huemer, "The Puzzle of Metacoherence," 1.

14 "External" in the sense that the statement is about something outside of the human mind. Compared to "internal" which I use to describe states inside of the human mind.

son it does seem to be a claim of knowledge of the truth of the belief. However, simply expressing the belief (even a categorical belief) that P is not a direct claim about an external reality. When one says, "I believe it is raining," what they are expressing is an internal claim about their mental state, and therefore not a claim about an external reality or about the truth of the belief. The believer is acknowledging a mental state, not directly claiming to know that the belief corresponds to the external world. They are, I maintain, statements about two categorically different things. For this reason, the statement "I believe it is raining" is categorically different from "it is raining."

This difference might be elucidated if we consider the case of human perception. Our senses are corrigible,[15] that is, we can be corrected about them. Our mental states of seeming or believing, however, are incorrigible. According to Louis Pojman, "beliefs are incorrigible for someone S if and only if it's not possible to show that person that he or she is mistaken."[16] This can be seen in cases of illusions; we seem to see things that are not actually there.

Imagine you find yourself in the middle of a vast desert. You swear you see a body of water in the distance. However, after miles of walking, the water slowly fades away so that you realize you were mistaken. You were in fact incorrect about the external claim that there was a body of water some miles away. Still though, the fact remains that it seemed to you that there was a body of water in the distance. This is because seeming is an incorrigible mental state, that is, we cannot be corrected about what

---

15 "Corrigible" is the idea that we may be corrected about a given mental state. This is distinguished from "fallible," which is the idea that any of our beliefs about the world could be false.

16 Louis Pojman, *What Can We Know?* (California. Wadsworth/ Thomson Learning, 2001), 101.

we seem to sense. So we can see that our internal mental states are categorically different than claims about an external reality.

The difference is that when someone claims that "it is raining," they are effectively corrected when conclusive data comes in that it is in fact not raining. They would now be currently incorrect about the fact that it is raining and retrospectively they were incorrect when they claimed it. However, when conclusive data comes in after one genuinely claims "I believe it is raining," they may change their belief rationally according to the evidence, but they are not corrected about the fact that they believed it before.

Since asserting a belief that P is about an entirely different "thing" than simply asserting that P, we can see that our second-order beliefs don't necessarily need to cohere to our first-order beliefs.

Oddly enough, I'm not the first to argue against *MR*. Allen Hazlett also argues against *MR* in a similar fashion:

> Suppose it is possible to reasonably believe p while suspending judgement about whether your belief constitutes knowledge. 'Since assertion is the canonical expression of belief,' it follows that, 'barring any unusual circumstances,' (Ibid.) someone could appropriately [epistemically] assert something of the form:
>
> p, but I suspend judgement about whether my belief constitutes knowledge.
>
> However, so the argument goes, it is impossible to appropriately assert (5) for the same reason that it is impossible to appropriately assert (6):

p, but I don't believe p.

[...]

As Huemer concedes, what is ultimately distinctive about (6) is not that it is impossible to appropriately assert it, but that it is impossible to rationally believe it. So Huemer's argument should be recast as appealing to the premise that it is impossible to rationally believe (5) for the same reason that it is impossible to rationally believe (6). But this premise is false. The reason it is impossible to rationally believe (6) is that you cannot believe it and end up believing something true.[17]

Hazlett identifies the same inaccuracy in Huemer's analogy listed earlier, albeit in more concise wording. While Huemer collapses statements (5) and (6), they are in fact not equal. This is because, while you cannot believe (6) and hold something true, you can in fact hold (5) and end up believing something true. What makes one wrong does not apply to the second, and thus Huemer's analogy fails.

Huemer is arguing to the conclusion—he gives an obviously contradictory statement (6 in Hazlett's version, and "it is raining but I don't know whether it is raining" in mine), and then equates it with an epistemically reasonable statement. Whether investigating Huemer's argument through my lens or Hazlett's, we can see that Huemer's appeal to the Moore-Paradox fails, and simply asserting a belief that P does not rationally commit one to the claim that one knows that P. The appeal to the Moore-

---

17 Allan Hazlett," Higher-Order Epistemic Attitudes and Intellectual Humility," *Episteme 9 no. 3. (2012): 15.*

paradox is the only argument given for MR, and because the analogy fails we can assume that there is no good reason to accept MR.

3. Does Asserting P Commit One to the View that One Knows P?

While we have seen that a statement of categorical belief such as "I believe that P" does not commit one to a claim of knowledge, the statement "it is true that P" does seem to commit one to that claim. Why is this so? This is because while "I believe that P" is a claim about an internal mental state, "it is true that P," or simply "P," does seem to be a claim about external reality. "It is true that it is raining" does in fact seem interchangeable with "it is raining." So given my explanation, it seems that the assertion of P does commit one, upon reflection to, the view that one knows P.

These cases become complicated due to our overextension of certain words like "knowledge" and "belief." The reality is that in our everyday language we often say things that do not reflect what we really mean epistemically. Belief, for example, is often merely implied. When we write papers in English class, instructors will often correct students and say something along the lines of, "You don't need to say you believe this is correct, because we know you believe it. It's your paper! It's redundant to say that you believe it."

Or imagine another scenario: you're watching the first inning of a baseball game with a friend when he turns to you and says, "the Angels are going to win." What is your first inclination? Do you think he's actually making a claim to know it, perhaps, by some insider information? Or that he merely believes that they will win? I hold that the more likely choice is the latter.

People often say statements that merely imply belief without explicitly claiming to have belief. I don't have the time here (or the background in linguistics) to go into much detail about the meaning and usage of words as signs, so I will leave the subject here. Nonetheless, since "the Angels are going to win" and "it is raining" are on the surface claims about external reality, the believers are, according to this evidence,[18] committed to the view that they know that the Angels are going to win, and that it is raining, respectively.

That being said, I suspect that, upon reflection and possibly with some probing, the speakers who utter common assertions like these that merely imply belief will eventually concede that they merely believe that the Angels will win, and therefore the believer will not have meant to make a knowledge claim. However, if they reflect and maintain that it is not simply a claim about their beliefs but that the Angels will in fact win, then that person is committed to the view that he knows that the Angels will win.

So it seems that asserting that P does not initially commit one to the view that one knows that P if that person reflects and maintains that it is not just a mental state and that it is in fact true that P, then he is committed to the view that he knows P. But simply asserting P without reflecting does not commit one to the view that he knows P, because as we have seen, belief is often implied and not stated.

I claim that if someone maintains an outright assertion that P after reflecting—then, and only then, is one

18 If there is no chance to question the speaker, we must take their statement at face value, that is, they're making a claim about external reality and therefore knowledge. However, if we have a chance to question them, we must withhold judgement until they either say it was implied belief or maintain their assertion.

committed to the view that he knows P.

I will now turn to the question of whether or not categorical belief that P requires an outright assertion that P. If it does, Huemer is right to conclude that all categorical beliefs entail a view that one knows that P. The corollary is that if categorical belief that P does not necessitate an outright assertion that P, then there is room for belief that does not rationally necessitate committing to the view that one knows that P.

4. Does Categorical Belief Necessitate Assertion?

I have argued that asserting and maintaining (after reflecting) that P is true does in fact commit one to the view that one knows P. The next question is, "does categorical belief in P necessitate an assertion that P?". If categorical belief does indeed necessitate assertion, then my argument stops there, as I've already argued that maintained assertion does commit one to the view that one knows P.

Fortunately, though, I don't think this is the case. Even Huemer concedes that categorical belief "is the attitude normally expressed by assertion."[19] So this alone would be enough to conclude that it does not necessitate assertion. Huemer might be correct in that it normally entails assertion. Most of the time we have a strong belief in something we are willing to assert it outright, and even when probed, we will maintain the assertion and, like I said before, in those instances, we are in fact committed to the view that we know it. But remember that Huemer's Metacoherence Requirement is, as a requirement, meant to apply to all categorical belief. Let's examine a different version of Huemer's "it is raining" example.

---

19 Huemer, "The Puzzle of Metacoherence," 2.

Imagine that you are sitting in your room writing a Philosophy thesis and your blinds are closed. You were outside only an hour ago and at that time it was raining. Your great-Aunt, who is older, calls and asks what the weather is like in California. Given the available evidence, you decide the best way to describe your attitude toward the question is to say you have a categorical belief that it is raining. That is, you have a strong belief—not complete certainty—but you are not tentative in asserting that you have a belief that it is raining, and it has both the attitude normally expressed by assertion, and the attitude required for knowledge.[20]

So the question is, does this belief that it is raining necessitate an assertion that it is raining? Again, I don't think it does. Imagine your Aunt continued to probe, and asked if you knew it was raining. It would be epistemically rational to reply, "I don't know whether it is raining, but I believe it is." According to Huemer, this response would be paradoxical, but I cannot see how this is the case. You are unsure about the external reality of the situation (or at least not sure enough to claim to know it), so you do not claim to know it. What you are sure of is your mental state and disposition towards whether it's raining, so you state a belief that it is raining. So, in cases like these, we are epistemically rational to have a categorical belief that P along with no assertion that P. Categorical belief of a proposition, then, does not necessitate an outright assertion of that proposition.

In many real life cases, this is the very reason for saying "I believe so-and-so." When we are asked about something that we are confident in, but not completely

---

20 I can only assume that Huemer would be fine with this case being a categorical belief because I am using the same belief he uses in his example, albeit with an elaboration on the details of how the believer came to believe it.

sure[21] of, we often concede with "I believe so" in order to avoid an outright assertion of a claim, and therefore to avoid committing to a knowledge claim. Simply uttering a belief that P does not commit one, on reflection, to the view that one knows P. What does commit one to the view that one knows P is an outright assertion that P.

Keep in mind that by "assertion" I do not mean an assertion of the fact that one has a belief. I am referring to an outright assertion of the statement without any reference to the mental state of belief. "I believe it is raining," therefore, is not an assertion of the proposition; it is merely an assertion that one has a certain kind of mental state. "It is raining," however, would be an outright assertion.

I feel that what I have presented so far is enough to show that categorical belief, even on Huemer's definition, does not always commit one to the view that we know that belief. Since there are cases in which we can be epistemically rational while being "meta-incoherent," we can see that the *MR* is not, by any definition, an epistemic requirement.

5. Does This View Require Infallibilism?

Some might understandably reply that my view entails fallibilism, that is, the view that we must have 100% certainty for knowledge. The objection might go something like: "If you are sure about your internal mental states but 'unsure' about the external reality, we can assume that we need to be sure, or 100% certain in our beliefs, to have knowledge. Infallibilism is the view that we need 100% certainty for knowledge, so your view entails infallibilism." Many oppose infallibilism because, if accepted, it

---

21 "Sure" makes my account sound like it hinges on infallibilism. I offer a reply to this observation in Section Five.

leads us to the conclusion that we actually "know" very little, as we are rarely 100% certain of things we claim to "know." However, I don't think this poses a forcible problem for my argument. This is because I can easily imagine a scenario in which a fallibilist[22] rationally claims not to know P while expressing a belief that P.

Let's imagine that Frank the fallibilist forms a belief that it is raining in a story similar to our earlier rain example. Frank is epistemically thorough, and he claims that he needs 90% credence that P before he claims to know that P. Now imagine Frank forming a categorical belief that "it is raining" because it was raining earlier, but he has no direct perception of the rain, and he's been indoors for a few hours. Frank has a lower requirement of credence for belief than he does knowledge, as many people do, and that requirement happens to be 85% credence. Since Frank has been inside a while, and he noticed earlier that the clouds were parting, he ascribes a credence of 87% to his categorical belief that "it is raining."

Frank would therefore assert a belief that it is raining without claiming to know that it is raining. So possibly, instead of saying, "Frank is not sure about whether P is true, but he is sure about his mental state of believing etc.," we could say, "Frank's credence in P does not meet his minimum requirement for knowledge, whatever that may be, but does meet his requirement for categorical belief." So we can see that Frank's fallibilism is fully consistent with the idea that we may be epistemically rational in not claiming to know our categorical beliefs even upon reflection. So MR does not hold as a requirement if fallibilism is the case.

It's worth noting that my reasoning applies both to subjective credence, or confidence in a proposition, and

---

22 A fallibilist is one who believes that we do not need 100% credence for knowledge.

also the evidential probability of a given proposition. My argument shows MR is not a requirement regardless of what the fallibilist requirements for knowledge and belief are, so long as the epistemic requirement for knowledge is higher than the requirement for belief.[23]

However, if infallibilism[24] is true, then *MR* does not hold as an epistemic requirement either. This is because if knowledge requires 100% credence, as infallibilism entails, and since according to Huemer categorical belief does not require 100% credence,[25] then we can easily imagine a case where a belief fills the categorical belief requirement without filling the knowledge requirement. Whatever belief is given a credence value that is required by categorical belief, but also lower than 100% certainty, would be a counterexample to MR if infallibilism is the case.

Since my argument does not necessitate either, I will not assume the truth of either fallibilism or infallibism and instead leave the question open. In either theory of these views of knowledge, metacoherence is not a necessary condition for epistemic rationality.

Conclusion

While metacoherence may very well describe a relationship that we find in many—possibly even a majority—of our categorical beliefs, it is not by any definition an epistemic requirement. This is because, as we have seen, asserting that P is categorically different than asserting a belief that P.

---

23 My view does not apply if our beliefs and knowledge share the same requirement. I respond to this objection in Section Six.

24 Infallibilism is the theory that knowledge requires 100% certainty in a proposition.

25 Huemer, "The Puzzle of Metacoherence," 3.

We have seen that belief that P and asserting P are two categorically different claims. Belief that P is merely a claim about one's internal mental states while asserting outright that P is a claim about external reality, and, for that reason, is a claim to knowledge. Since these are statements about two categorically different things, it is epistemically acceptable to have second-order beliefs that do not cohere with our first-order beliefs, and therefore we can be epistemically rational in having a belief without claiming to know it.

Moreover, we have seen that a categorical belief that P does not necessitate an assertion that P. This is because standards for categorical belief that P may rationally be lower than the standards to claim knowledge that P. This is because the idea that knowledge-level justification is required for belief leads to unwanted consequences—that even "being of the opinion that P" commits us, upon reflection, to the view that we know that P—since belief that P, thinking that P, and being of the opinion that P, are equal epistemic states. This difference in requirements elucidates the possibility of having epistemically justified categorical beliefs without necessitating the claim that we know that they are true.

We have also seen that my theory of meta-incoherence is compatible with either a fallibilistic or an infallibilistic theory of knowledge justification.

I will conclude that we may be epistemically rational in denying that we know propositions that we categorically believe. Since there are rational exceptions to it, Huemer's Metacoherence Requirement is not an epistemic requirement at all.

Bibliography

Chivers, Laura. "Blindsight and Consciousness." Serendip Studio.
    http://serendip.brynmawr.edu/exchange/node/1676 Date
    Published: January 3rd, 2008. Date accessed: December 2nd,
    2013.

Hazlett, Allan. "Higher-Order Epistemic Attitudes and Intellectual
    Humility." Epistime vol. 9, no. 3. (2012): 1-31.

Huemer, Michael. "The Puzzle of "Metacoherence."1-4. Philosophy
    and Phenomenological Research, LLC. Vol. 82, Issue 1. (2011):
    1-21.

Myers-Schulz, Blake, and Eric Schwitzgebel. "Knowing That P
    Without Believing That P." *Noûs* 47, no. 2. (2013): 1-27.

Pojman, Louis. What Can We Know? Second Edition. California:
    Wadsworth/Thomson Learning. 2001.

Radford, Colin. "Knowledge---By Examples." Analysis 27, no. 1.
    (1966).

Schumacher, Ralph. "Blindsight and the Role of the Phenomenal
    Qualities of Visual Perceptions." Philosophy of Mind.
    http://www.bu.edu/wcp/Papers/Mind/MindSchu.htm
Date accessed: December 4th, 2013.

Weiskrantz, Lawrence. Blindsight. Second Edition. New York: Oxford
    University Press. 2009.

*Ryan Scheuring is a fourth-year undergraduate student
in philosophy at Chapman University in Southern California. Along with studying philosophy, he plans to earn
minors in writing and rhetoric and psychology. While his
work focuses on epistemology, he also writes in applied
ethics and philosophy of religion.*

Frege and Fodor

Methodology in
Cognitive Science and Analytic Philosophy

Maxwell Marler
Concordia University, Montreal, Canada

In this essay, I will show that Fodor's guiding insight in *Concepts: Where Cognitive Science Went Wrong* is the distinction between epistemological and metaphysical theories of concepts. Drawing from chapter one of *Concepts,* I will first give a sketch of Fodor's view that much of cognitive science is methodologically bankrupt insofar as it builds a theory of concepts on the basis of concept use, and not on the basis of a concept's objective nature as a mental particular; a concept that is independent of one's epistemic capacities. In what I hope will shed light on Fodor's own position, I will look at Frege's *Grundlagen der Arithmetik* and primarily focus on his concept of 'Number' as analytic/*a-priori*, his criticism of subjectivist accounts of Number, and finally elucidate what Michael Dummett coined the 'linguistic turn,' which is what I think Fodor is really responding to in his critique of cognitive science. I will then argue that while some have understood Frege through Dummett's reading of section 46 of the *Grundlagen*, where he reads Frege as saying concepts should be understood in terms of their use, there are good reasons for thinking that the 'linguistic turn' is not Frege's. This will show that the spirit of Fodor's text, insofar as it seeks a cognitive science that treats concepts ontologically, maps quite nicely onto the guiding methodological and metaphysical principles set out by Frege at the *beginning* of the *Grundlagen*.

Frege is a strict externalist[1] when it comes to concepts; a concept's nature is quite independent of one's capacity for such a concept. When attempting to secure the concept of Number itself, Frege excludes any account of Number that is contingent on human capacities. This prohibition extends to seeing Number as a) the property of external things,[2] b) a subjective idea one applies to experience,[3] c) a by-product of intuition,[4] and d) something learned during development by virtue of induction.[5] While these might be seen as harsh restrictions, his initial elucidation of the ethos of his text in the introduction, in which he states the rationale that guides his text, is quite indicative of his commitment to fix the nature of concepts in a way that does justice to their objective, external, and overarchingly *metaphysical role* within the

---

1 By externalism I mean the view that the objective nature of any concept C exists independently of a cognisor's ability to understand the concept, even if said cognisor uses the concept; the concept of Number for instance, Frege would argue, has an ontological status independent of a cognisor's capacity to use it. This view is still held by cognitive scientists today insofar as the data shows any alternative is implausible. See Alvin Goldman's Goldman, Alvin I.. *Philosophical applications of cognitive science.* Boulder: Westview Press, 1993.

2 Gottlob, Frege, *The Foundations of Artihmetic; A Logico-Mathematical Enquiry Into the Concept of Number* (Evanston: Northwestern University Press, 1968), 21.

3 Ibid.,§26.

4 Ibid., §40.

5 Ibid., §9.

bounds of "the laws of logic".[6] He doesn't say much about what this metaphysics is in the *Grundlagen*; he hints towards Platonism in stating that objects need not be physical.[7] For example, Frege argues in the introduction that while mathematical skill may be developed over time, this question of capacity for mathematical thought is quite a different question than the ontological question; mathematical capacity "does not prove that numbers are formed in some peculiarly mechanical way, as sand, say, is formed out of quartz granules".[8]

In critiquing different methods of assessing the concept of number, Frege describes what he takes to be a psychological explication of Number, that is, any explanation of the concept of Number that is constituted by an *empirical description* such as the concept of Number as a development over history, the physiology of human beings as grounding the concept of Number, as well as any view of Number as contained in 'mental pictures' or 'ideas'.[9] Frege is clear that such a 'psychological' methodology is unfounded, and this is shown by the first of his three fundamental principles of his enquiry: "always to separate sharply the psychological from the logical, the subjective from the objective".[10] What method does Frege have in mind? As mentioned earlier, Frege sought the objective nature of the concept of Number, so anything that characterises Number as part of a 'pebble and gingerbread arithmetic' will simply not do insofar as it characterises Number as a by-product of "inductive inference".[11] Frege wished to ground the definition of the

---

6 Ibid., IV.

7 Ibid., §61.

8 Ibid., IV.

9 Ibid., IV.

10 Ibid., X.

11 Ibid., §10.

concept of Number as achievable 'analytic/a-priori' and indeed believed he had succeeded in coherently proving this with the *Grundlagen*; however, his discussion in the introduction should lead one to think that a definition wouldn't exhaust the nature of the concept. A definition is epistemic in a way that Number, ontologically speaking, is not.[12] This will become clearer in the next section where I will illustrate what Dummett has hailed 'the linguistic turn' in section 46.

We all know what happens in section 46: Frege argues that it would "shed some light" on the analysis of the concept of Number to "consider [it] within the context of a judgement which brings out its basic use".[13] In what Dummett calls 'the linguistic turn,' Frege attempts to see Number as "something asserted of a concept," and only understandable, as the second guiding principle of the *Grundlagen* states, "in the context of a proposition".[14] So, perhaps, one can look at the use of a concept, but does that tell us anything about the concept of Number itself? Frege's move captures what Dummett called a change from seeking the meaning of concepts in their objective form, and attempting to understand concepts within their linguistic context; hence, the dictum: "the meaning of a concept is constituted in its use." What I want to argue is that one should not conclude that Frege is in anyway throwing away the notion of concepts as objective, and even Dummett acknowledges this. While the 'linguistic turn' is a methodological innovation, it is not, in fact, a substantive methodological decision that resembles a paradigmatic shift in Frege's metaphysics, as the decision is more of a pragmatic consideration one

---

12 Ibid., §108.

13 Ibid., §46.

14 Ibid., X.

can embark on in attempting to approach the nature of number.[15] This is where Fodor comes in: the nature of concepts should be sought within metaphysical considerations and not epistemic ones. What does this mean? And how does it relate to Frege? I will show in the next section that Frege's "solution to the difficulty" has, in the eyes of Fodor, led to fundamental axiomatic shortcoming in cognitive science as a research program.

In chapter one of Fodor's *Concepts*, Fodor comes clean about just how far-reaching his book intends to be. The notion of concepts as capacities, which Fodor claims underlies "much of our current cognitive science and practically all of our current philosophy of the mind," is built on a 'metaphysical subtext'.[16] Fodor's key idea in this chapter is that fixing the objective nature of concepts, one of the key aspects of any successful cognitive science, should be guided by metaphysical considerations rather than epistemic considerations: "what concepts you have is conceptually and metaphysically independent of what epistemic capacities you have".[17] In reacting to what he labels as a view of concepts as capacities, one which much of cognitive science is said to hold, Fodor advances his view of concepts as "mental particulars": "[to] follow this course is in effect to assume that it's OK for theorizing about the nature of concepts to precede theorizing about concept possession".[18] Fodor's assumption is that cognitive science needs an account of concepts, and such an account dictates the nature of research in cognitive

---

15 See *Origins of Analytical Philosophy* by Michael Dummett,1993. and *Michael Dummett on Frege* on the Philosophy Bites podcast, October 7th 2010.

16 Jerry A. Fodor, *Concepts: Where Cognitive Science Went Wrong* (Oxford: Clarendon Press, 1998), 2-4.

17 Ibid., 6.

18 Ibid., 3-6.

science. Insofar as cognitive science sees concepts as capacities, they fail to see what concepts actually are, which is what Fodor argues are mental particulars. Seeing concepts epistemically is, Fodor argues, "where cognitive went wrong." Fodor's assumption, I would argue, is Fregian in spirit, since Fodor has realised that dispositional analysis, the kind of analysis that Frege opposed to in the *Grundlagen*, is endemic to cognitive science, just as it was for uncovering the foundations of arithmetic, insofar as it fails to secure objectivity. Cognitive science should not only be concerned with the use of concepts, but also with concepts themselves.

If one fixes a view of concepts based on their use, then one has not fixed their metaphysical conditions and objective nature. While Frege argues on a pragmatic basis that one should look at concepts based on their use, if one sees the spirit of his work as grounded in the understanding of the difference between the objective and the subjective, then is there not a contradiction between Frege's solution and his goal? If one sees Frege as an externalist with respect to concepts, i.e., the constitution of concepts exists independently of human beings, then I would argue that Fodor and Frege agree that: *looking at a concept A's use does not fix concept A's nature.* One need not be a Platonist to see the importance of an externalist view of concepts in cognitive science. In using an analogy, atomistic concepts can be understood in light of Platonic forms, as they exist independently of their instantiation, and by extension, fixing their essence is a consideration quite distinct from fixing the conditions of a concept's use, or even one's idea of a concept. Furthermore, the form of objective concepts for Plato shape the nature of judgements in the same way that concepts as external mental particulars shape propositional attitudes, thoughts, and beliefs. Even Socrates knew that the only thing Meno's knowledge of geometry revealed was that certain seemingly *a priori* concepts could be accessed through recollection, but he didn't argue that the nature of the concepts was constituted in this recollection or demonstration of this knowledge. However, the meaning of concepts as external in Fodor's sense is quite distinct from what Frege means by external if Frege is to be interpreted as a Platonist. I would argue, however, that Fodor's notion of externality of concepts within the mind, along with the notion that many concepts are innate, can be understood in light of Frege's guiding principles.

While Fodor is, I would argue, an externalist about concepts in the basic sense where concepts exist independently and "prior to understanding how we know what it is," there is an obvious sense in which Frege would not argue, I think, that "the natural home of a theory of concepts is part of a theory of mental states".[19] Frege did hold that concepts could be non-physical, which is something that would fly in the face of cognitive science's ethos on better days. However, maybe there is a methodological point to what Fodor is saying that is perhaps similar to what Frege had in mind with his supposed "linguistic turn." This methodological point might even be a true help to cognitive science. While concepts may be prior to our thoughts about them in the same sense that Number would be for Frege, and furthermore, while their true nature might not be best characterised by their use, there is a methodological advantage to cognitive science in contrast to a certain view of analytic philosophy that makes the approach Fodor takes sensible.

If one takes the view that a strand of analytic philosophy, what some have labelled "standard analytic epistemology" (SAE), promotes the idea that one can uncover

---

19 Ibid., 6.

the nature of concepts like "Justification" by appeal to reason or a "reflective equilibrium." If one considers the criticism of the SAE program as an unsuccessful methodology, then one can see how it follows that someone like Fodor can, on the one hand, agree with the metaphysical subtext of much of SAE, yet disagree methodologically with SAE while remaining a cognitive scientist and studying mental states.[20] While Frege might be correct about the externality of concepts like Number and their metaphysical role, I would argue that philosophy, science, and, more generally, humanity (except for Ernest Sosa[21]) is at a loss as to how to access the *a priori* through the methods of SAE. While there seems to be a universality to the notion of Number as well as an *a priori* character to it, one must resort to a science of instantiation of mental states in getting closer to uncovering something about the objectivity of concepts as well as other seemingly universal concepts. Frege was clearly aware of the difficulty of *a priori* elucidation, and this is shown by his choice to assess something even Fodor would argue is too external to "Thought" in the hopes of uncovering the nature of concepts: language. The idea is that, while Fodor does agree with SAE that concepts are in some sense *a priori*/external, he would disagree that the method of achieving and understanding concepts is introspection while also disagreeing with the view that a dispositional analysis, something he claims is critical to cognitive science today, is the correct way of attaining concepts.

---

20 See: Bishop and Trout for a criticisms of SAE in: Michael A. Bishop and J. D. Trout, *Epistemology and the Psychology of Human Judgment* (New York: Oxford University Press, 2005); and Joshua Michael Knobe, Experimental Philosophy (Oxford: Oxford University Press, 2008).

21 See: Sosa's chapter *A Defense of the Use of Intuitions in Philosophy,* in *Stich and His Critics* 2005.

Thus, there is a virtue in Fodor's approach. While the analytic philosopher might cringe, a cognitive science that looks closely at the role of concepts as mental particulars and parts of mental states might give an account, and be the only approach capable of giving such an account, of concepts as instantiated across cultures, and even species, and that partially preserves the non-psychological nature of Frege's mission in the *Grundlagen* insofar as concepts themselves are independent of the cognisor. The goal, for Frege, was to get an account of the essence concepts that are non-psychologistic, and I would argue that insofar as Fodor seeks a cognitive science that provides metaphysical account of concepts, there may be more similarity at play than some might think. But in the same way that Frege sought concepts in their objective sense and resorted an approach that considered their use, Fodor is also looking at concepts ontologically whist also resorting to a cognitive science approach in which one studies concepts *within the context of their instantiation as mental states*. There might be a universality to the concept of number, and, as Fodor points out, one would be mistaken in looking at the concept as a disposition. However, one can be a metaphysician about concepts and still remain a scientist by looking at the way concepts are instantiated in mental states in the same way that one can be a metaphysician about the concept of number while resorting to studying the role of number in the context of language.

Bibliography

Bishop, Michael A., and J. D. Trout. *Epistemology and the Psychology of Human Judgment*. New York: Oxford University Press, 2005.

Dummett, Michael. Origins of Analytical Philosophy. Cambridge: Harvard University Press, 1994.

Dummett, Michael. *Origins of Analytical Philosophy*. Cambridge, Mass.: Harvard University Press, 1994.

Fodor, Jerry A. *Concepts: Where Cognitive Science Went Wrong*. Oxford: Clarendon Press, 1998.

Frege, Gottlob. *The Foundations of Arithmetic; A Logico-Mathematical Enquiry into the Concept of Number*. 2nd ed. Evanston: Northwestern University Press, 1968.

Goldman, Alvin I. *Philosophical Applications of Cognitive Science*. Boulder: Westview Press, 1993.

Knobe, Joshua Michael. *Experimental Philosophy*. Oxford: Oxford University Press, 2008.

Murphy, Dominic and Bishop, Michael A. "A Defense of the Use of Intuitions in Philosophy." In Stitch and his Critics. Chichester: Wiley-Blackwell, 2009.

Maxwell Marler is an undergraduate student in his final semester of a Bachelor of Arts in honours philosophy at Concordia University in Montreal, Quebec. By pursuing graduate studies that will focus on both the work of analytic philosophers and cognitive scientists, Maxwell intends to continue his research into the nature of concepts. In this line of inquiry, Maxwell hopes to detail the tension between causal accounts of concept acquisition and the notion that cognisors acquire logico-mathematical concepts, while also working on how logico-mathematical concepts, once acquired, fit into theory construction in the sciences.

Freud, the Connection Principle, and Token-Identity

Daniel Scott Spina
University of California, Berkeley,
Berkeley, USA

Freud, the Connection Principle, and Token-Identity[1]

It is frequently said that unconscious intentional states, like beliefs and desires, become conscious.[2] Moreover, to say that a desire "arrives" in consciousness seems to entail that both the unconscious desire and the conscious desire are identical; however, this commonsense way of talking about the unconscious raises substantial philosophical questions. First, what notion of identity do we use when we employ phrases like "her belief came to consciousness"? Second, what, if anything, justifies this usage? How does our way of talking about the unconscious

1 An earlier draft of this paper was written during Professor John Searle's seminar "Consciousness" at UC Berkeley. I would like to thank Professor Searle for his insightful comments on an earlier draft. I would also like to thank Sophie Dandelet and Katia Moles for their extensive comments on many previous drafts. This paper was made possible by all of their patient guidance and encouraging support.

2 Although this paper will deal exclusively with intentional states, much of the same remarks can be given for other mental states.

inform and delimit our notions of mental and ontological sameness?

In his essay, "The Unconscious," Sigmund Freud discusses two possible ontologies of the unconscious mind. In an attempt to briefly characterize a fully-fledged metaphysical picture of repression, he carefully put forward the following disjunction: either an unconscious state is ontologically identical to its conscious correlate, or an unconscious state is entirely distinct from its conscious correlate.

Nearly a century later, John Searle's discussion of Freud and the unconscious seems to entail some version of the second Freudian ontology. Searle argues that all unconscious states are dispositions to cause conscious ones, and as a result, these dispositions are ontologically different in kind from their conscious occurrences. Nonetheless, Searle thinks that the analogies we use to discuss the relation between the unconscious and conscious mind have "a harmless use" as long as we understand that identical mental states can be ontologically distinct.[3]

However, Jerry Fodor and Ernest Lepore present an objection to this view of the relation between the conscious mind and the unconscious. They argue for the following possibility: an unconscious state could lose an essential attribute when it comes to consciousness, and thus come to consciousness as an entirely different state.[4] This unconscious state would not be token-identical to its conscious correlate since it comes to consciousness as a completely different state. Such a possibility would rule out exactly what Searle's analysis requires: all uncon-

3 John R. Searle "The Connection Principle and the Ontology of the Unconscious: A Reply to Fodor and Lepore" *Philosophy and Phenomenological Research* 54, no. 4 (1994): 855.

4 Jerry Fodor, and Ernest Lepore. "What Is the Connection Principle?," *Philosophy and Phenomenological Research* 54, no. 4 (1994): 837-845.

scious states must be able to cause their token-correlates in consciousness.

In this paper, I argue that once confusions surrounding our commonsense conception of the unconscious are exposed, Fodor and Lepore's objection appears to suffer from similar errors. These mistakes result from the common language we use to describe distinct concepts; in doing so, we have conflated two independent notions of identity that have intimate ties with Freud's picture of the unconscious. Using the dialectic between Searle and Fodor and Lepore, I argue that an escape from this confused picture requires some distinction between what can be called ontological identity and mental-token-identity. I agree with Searle that part of getting clear about the unconscious will be to understand that the metaphorical language that comes out of Freud's analysis has led to an "incoherent picture." I think it is also important to understand *how* the everyday language that makes the unconscious intelligible has led to confusions surrounding ontological identity and mental-token identity.

I will begin by providing an overview of some of the more neutral terms that these writers use to discuss the unconscious. I will then explain Freud's brief hypothesis in "The Unconscious" and its relation to the way we conceptualize the unconscious today. Next, I will outline Searle's argument for the *Connection Principle* to clarify its scope. Further, I will evaluate Fodor and Lepore's objection to the Connection Principle, and argue that it too hides unsubstantiated ontological claims. Last, I will use Tim Crane's notion of unconscious belief to motivate an argument that preserves the Connection Principle and gives a point of departure for revising the "comes to consciousness" vocabulary.

Intentional States, Ontological identity and Token Identity

Integral to the project of understanding how the same mental state comes to consciousness is to get precise on exactly *how* these mental states are the same in the first place. In order to get clear on the different ways that these states can be said to be identical, I will first discuss intentional states and three specific ways in which we call intentional states "the same".

Beliefs and desires are paradigm cases of intentional mental states. According to John Searle, an intentional state is individuated by two essential elements: its intentional mode and its intentional content. Intentional modes, like belief and desire, are the attitudes that a subject takes toward some way the world is or could be. The intentional content is what the belief or desire is about; it is the subject matter of the attitude. For example, a belief 'that it will rain' has as its intentional mode belief, and an intentional content that 'it will rain'.[5]

There are many ways that mental states are said to be the same. I will focus specifically on three ways. Perhaps, the most familiar way intentional states are said to be the same is through mental-type-identity.[6] For the purposes of this paper, states that have both their intentional mode and their intentional content in common are type-identical states. So, my belief that 'it will snow in Munich' and your belief that 'it will snow in Munich' are type-

5 Following Searle, for shorthand I will abbreviate a mental state with intentional mode 'S' and intentional content 'p' as S(p).

6 It is crucial to notice that I am diverting sharply from some traditional uses of type-identity where type-identity is taken to simply suggest two mental states that have their intentional mode in common.

identical. One helpful mark of type-identity is that it can be used to discuss interpersonal mental sameness. Your mental states can be type-identical to mine.

A second sort of identity, the sort that this paper will be most concerned with, is mental-token-identity.[7] Contrary to type-identity, this kind of identity is used to discuss mental particulars within a single subject, and so cannot be used in discussions of interpersonal mental sameness. The subjective nature of the mind rules out sharing the same mental-token. In the previous example, we shared a belief that 'it will snow in Munich' insofar as we had two separate mental tokens of the same mental type. Since this kind of identity is what this paper will discuss, an uninformative definition is what is best for now—a mental state is token identical to another if the first mental state is the same mental particular as the other.

The third notion of identity that will be vital for our discussion is ontological identity. Two entities that exist at the same time and take up the exact same space (spatio-identical particulars) will be ontologically identical. Ontological identity is an extremely controversial notion that requires a much more careful discussion than I can give here. Furthermore, the ontology of the mind and how it might be reduced to the workings of the brain is another extremely controversial issue. I will not engage in any discussion of the brain here. For the purposes of this paper, I assume that the ontological identity of a mental state must respect a basic distinction between mental events and mental states.[8] States are persisting qualities. For instance, when I say that the building is not earthquake-proof, I am ascribing a property to the build-

---

7 Hereafter referred to as token-identity.

8 Matthew Soteriou. "Content And The Stream Of Consciousness." *Philosophical Perspectives* 21, no. 1 (2007): 547.

ing that persists for as long as the building stands unreinforced. On the other hand, an event is something that an object undergoes. When the building starts to crumble and eventually falls to the ground during an earthquake, the destruction of the building is an event. Beliefs are examples of mental states, and daydreaming is a good example of a mental event. Daydreaming takes place over a specific amount of time; it does not make sense to say that someone had a particular daydream and that this was a persisting property of them. On the other hand, I do not need to mention any specific amount of time to ascribe a belief. A particular belief state obtains over a period of time, but does not need any particular period of time *to* obtain. Since events, or occurrences will never be ontologically identical with states, members of one ontological category will never be members of the other category; these categories are mutually exclusive.[9]

Ultimately, I will suggest that the second and third notions of identity are importantly distinct. At first, this thesis looks unintuitive. One may object straight away that mental-tokens are merely a more specific subset of ontological-tokens. That is, ontological identity is just a more general relation than mental-token-identity. I want to argue that in some cases, at least some particulars fall under the extension of mental-token-identical states and yet cannot be ontologically identical. Once this distinction is made more intuitive, it will form the crux of the argument against "coming to consciousness" vocabularies, which seem to conflate ontological identity and token-identity.

---

9 In this paper, I will sometimes use "state" to refer broadly to any mental particular; I will indicate as clearly as possible if I intend the narrow ontological category in any particular discussion.

Freud on the Unconscious

Freud also carefully considered different notions of 'sameness' that we use to talk about the unconscious and conscious mind. Freud first briefly discusses two accounts of mental ontology in his essay "The Unconscious":

> When a psychical act...is transposed from the [unconscious] into the [conscious] system, are we to suppose that this transposition involves a fresh record-as it were, a second registration-of the idea in question, which may thus be situated as well in a fresh psychical locality...or are we rather to believe that the transposition consists in a change in the state of the idea, a change involving the same material and occurring in the same locality?[10]

This passage gives two views of what it is to have an unconscious state become conscious. On the first conception, mental states that are conscious are "fresh records" of the unconscious. That is, conscious and unconscious states are distinct. On the second view, an unconscious state comes to consciousness; the exact same state "arrives" in consciousness after crossing the border between the unconscious and the conscious mind. Freud points out that an informed choice of either account would require a clear explanation of not only mental sameness, but a scientific account of the brain. This strongly suggests that Freud is referring to ontological identity in this passage, an understanding of identity that would be (putatively) found in the physical workings of the brain.

Although Freud's brief discussion of mental ontology

---

10 Sigmund Freud. "The Unconscious" (1915) reprinted in *Freud: Complete Works*. ed. Ivan Smith, 2011. 2998.

adopts concrete and scientific terms, other passages notoriously employ highly metaphorical language. He calls these analogies "spatial" comparisons—analogies involving entities moving about in places located in space. Although these metaphors lack precise language, they give enormous expressive power to descriptions of the otherwise impenetrable unconscious. Freud later describes his hypothesis of the Conscious, Preconscious and Unconscious mind with such an analogy. He writes:

> The crudest idea of these systems is the most convenient for us– a spatial one. Let us therefore compare the system of the unconscious to a large entrance hall, in which the mental impulses jostle one another like separate individuals. Adjoining this entrance hall there is a second, narrower, room– a kind of drawing-room - in which consciousness, too, resides. But on the threshold between these two rooms a watchman performs his function: he examines the different mental impulses, acts as a censor, and will not admit them into the drawing-room if they displease him.[11]

Freud's analogy describes that an unconscious state becomes conscious just as a person passes through one room into another. Specifically, once a mental state token arrives in the next room it is conscious. Already, this analogy feels intuitive to fit it into the arrival theory of the unconscious. That is, the analogy bears resemblance to that ontology; it is almost compulsory to think that just as the same token-state passes from room to room, the ontology of that state is undergoing a similar process. Because most of these analogies feature a single spatio-

11 Sigmund Freud. "Introductory Lectures on Psycho-Analysis" (1916-1917) reprinted in *Freud: Complete Works*. ed. Ivan Smith, 2011. 3369.

temporal particular moving about between the unconscious and the conscious mind, it is hard *not* to think that the physical ontology of this process might also somehow be doing something similar. However, this is the opposite of what Freud intended. Freud's use of an analogy in the second passage sharply contrasts with the more concrete language that he used in the first, suggesting that he too wanted to independently conceptualize different kinds of mental sameness. Freud later called his entrance hall analogy "crude," "fantastic" and even "impermissible in a scientific account".[12] Freud was already aware of exactly how these analogies could mislead, and his different descriptions in these two passages show that. More specifically, Freud's hyperawareness of the distinct rhetorical situations surrounding these two types of identity manifests itself in his usage of abstract language in one passage and careful concrete language in the other, suggesting that he is fully aware of our predisposition to let these spatial analogies delimit our conception of a scientific mental ontology.

Our common way of speaking about the unconscious has come to conflate these two accounts exactly in the way that Freud foresaw. Because analogies that make the unconscious intelligible typically contain a single spatiotemporal particular, like the analogy above, the vocabulary steeped in these analogies suggests the arrival view of the unconscious. In this way, phrases like 'comes to consciousness' are commonly taken to immediately suggest the arrival view and hence make unsubstantiated ontological claims. Such phrases already presuppose that an unconscious state will be ontologically identical to its conscious correlate, but when we use these phrases we typically do not justify that usage. As we will see later, the

---

12 Ibid., 3369.

same justification is lacking in Fodor and Lepore's objection to Searle, indicating that these analogies are working to substantiate their assumption of the arrival ontology as well. But first, I will discuss Searle's analysis of the unconscious.

Searle on Unconscious Intentionality and the Connection Principle

Searle argues that any unconscious intentional state must be "possibly conscious".[13] That is, an unconscious intentional state must be a state that a subject could have consciously. In order to get clear on his claim, it is important to understand the distinction between contingently unconscious states and essentially unconscious states. As an example of a contingently unconscious state, take Susan's unconscious belief that she is six feet tall. Now that Susan is asleep, her belief is unconscious, but it can become conscious when I ask her how tall she is when she wakes up. If her belief is repressed, she may not be able to have it consciously without the help of a psychotherapist. Nonetheless, her belief is contingently unconscious, even though it is not currently conscious, it could potentially become conscious.

On the other hand, essentially unconscious states would be unconscious by definition. Even with the help of a psychotherapist, these states could never become conscious, since it would be in their very nature to be unconscious. In other words, these states would not be the *kind* of thing that could ever be conscious. Searle calls these states unconscious "in principle".[14] Searle's thesis

---

13 John R. Searle, *The Rediscovery of the Mind*, (Cambridge: MIT, 1992), 160-161.
14 Ibid., 161-2.

requires that essentially unconscious states cannot exist. This thesis is called the Connection Principle (hereafter referred to as CP). The CP maintains that a state can be *contingently* unconscious, but not *essentially* unconscious.

Searle argues for the CP by demonstrating that essentially unconscious states would not have "aspectual shapes."[15] The aspectual shapes of an intentional state is the *way* that something is conceived of in the mind. All intentional states have aspectual shape since it is impossible to think of something without thinking about it in some way or another. This idea can be illustrated with an intuitive example: think of the current president of the United States. How exactly does he show up in your thought? Perhaps, you are thinking of the word 'Obama,' or maybe you think of the words 'the first black president,' or maybe just a recent photograph of him comes to mind. What is clear is that thinking of anything at all requires thinking about it in some way. In Searle's terms, thinking occurs under some aspectual shape or other.

Searle asks, how can one think of the current president *as* "Obama" or *as* "the first black president of the U.S." *unconsciously*? He thinks that this is impossible since at the unconscious level, one is not conceiving in any way at all. Since unconscious states cannot have aspectual shapes *as* unconscious, and since all intentional states necessarily require aspectual shapes, unconscious states can only be dispositional states, that is, potentials to cause a conscious state with some determinate aspectual shape. For example, to say that Jane has an unconscious intentional state with aspectual shape β is to say that Jane has a disposition to have a conscious state with

---

15 Ibid., 156-7.

aspectual shape β.[16] In this way, an unconscious state S(p) is token-identical to the conscious state that it causes with the intentional mode S and content p. However, the unconscious state is a disposition, and the conscious state is a realization of that disposition, an occurrence. In this way, states can be token-identical even if they are ontologically distinct.

Establishing the Possibility of Essentially Unconscious States: An Objection to the Connection Principle

Yet it is at first unclear what it means for every intentional state to be potentially conscious. In their objection to Searle, Fodor and Lepore ask whether all unconscious intentional states must be type-identical to some conscious state, or whether they must have the ability to cause the exact same mental token in consciousness. they consider both interpretations of the CP: Either (1) Any intentional state must be a *type* of state that a subject could have as a conscious thought; or (2) every *token* intentional state must be a possible conscious state. Importantly, (2) is a much stronger claim since (1) does not entail (2), but (2) entails (1).

Take, for example, George and Jane. Let's say that George has an *unconscious* state S(p), and Jane has the same *conscious* state S(p). These states have the same intentional mode and intentional content, so they are type-identical. Both states are consistent with (1). The state is a conscious type, since Jane is consciously enjoying S(p). If all that the CP requires is that unconscious intentional states must be type-identical with some conscious state, then it is irrelevant whether George's state could ever be

16 Ibid., 158.

conscious.

Yet, on the stronger construal, the CP requires token-sameness. This would mean that every token must be capable of generating itself in consciousness, a stronger thesis that quickly runs into possible objections. In the previous example, when George's state becomes conscious—whether through prompting, or through psychotherapy—if his state was *essentially unconscious,* it would *not* be token-identical to his unconscious state. Fodor and Lepore consider the possibility that George's state S(p) could lose an essential attribute when it becomes conscious, and might come to consciousness as $S_2(p)$, a state with a different intentional mode.[17] If Searle asserts that all token intentional states are possibly conscious, then the existence of an essentially unconscious state would provide a counterexample to CP. I now turn to Fodor and Lepore's argument for this possibility.

The Argument for an Essentially Unconscious State

Fodor and Lepore purport to establish the possibility of an essentially unconscious state with the following argument, which contains premises that are (so far) consistent with Searle's account:

1. If you change the intentional mode of a state you change the state that it is (intentional mode change will result in token change)

2. There exist some changes in causal powers that are sufficient for a change in intentional mode

---

17 Jerry Fodor and Ernest Lepore. "What Is the Connection Principle?," *Philosophy and Phenomenological Research 54,* no. 4 (1994): 845.

3. Bringing a state into conscious awareness can change its causal powers (consciousness is not epiphenomenal)

4. Thus, it is possible that making a state conscious could change its intentional mode (2,3)

5. So essentially unconscious states, states that change their intentional mode when they become conscious could possibly exist (1,4)

In short, because a state changes in causal powers when it becomes conscious, and because some changes in causal powers are sufficient for changes in intentional mode, a state could change its intentional mode when it came to consciousness and thus be essentially unconscious. Thus, even if all unconscious states are the *type* of state that could be conscious, this is not the case for all possible *token* states.[18]

The most vital question for my discussion of this objection will be the following: why should we think of the essentially unconscious state S(p) and its conscious correlate $S_2(p)$ as the same state? In other words, it is unclear why Fodor and Lepore think that the conscious correlate is identical to its unconscious disposition. But their objection *depends* on it. Given that they try to track the ontology of a mental state using functional powers, Fodor and Lepore seem to be trying to posit the possibility of an unconscious state that is ontologically identical to its conscious correlate, but is not token-identical. That is the very objection to Searle: not all unconscious states, when conscious, have the same intentional mode.

In order for the Connection Principle to resist Fodor

---

18 Ibid., 842.

and Lepore's objection, I will argue that it either must give decisive reasons to reject the claim that some changes in causal powers are sufficient for changes in intentional mode, or it must somehow show that their use of ontological sameness is unsubstantiated. I will take each strategy up in turn.

How do Causal Powers Determine Intentional Modes?

Premise two asserts that a difference in causal powers can sometimes amount to a difference in intentional mode. This premise assumes that the behavioral and psychological causes and effects of a given mental state *determine* (in part) the intentional mode of a mental state. As support for this claim, Fodor and Lepore allege that (a) "the mental kind of a mental state is (at least in part) determined by its causal powers." They believe that it follows from (a) that (b) "at least some differences in causal powers are sufficient for at least some differences of mental kind".[19] In order to see how claim (b) follows from claim (a), it is important to see exactly what Fodor and Lepore mean when they assert that a state's causal powers *determine* its intentional mode.

At first glance, this claim runs contrary to common-sense intuitions about the mind. A state can change its causal powers without changing the state it is. For example, when I become tired over the course of the day, I may be less likely to act on my desires. Nonetheless, the desire I have while wide-awake could be identical to the desire I have just before I go to bed. Even a drastic change in the causal powers of my desire is entirely consistent with it still being the desire it is. In Searle's reply to Fodor and

19 Ibid., 841.

Lepore's objection, he also finds this thesis implausible, calling it "entirely out of the question".[20]

Given intuitions like these, one plausible reading of this claim is epistemological. The causal powers of a state justify ascribing certain mental states to others; or better, we understand what certain attitudes are based on the typical effects they cause.[21] For example, when a friend orders the curry rather than the beef tartare, I am justified in ascribing the desire for curry to him. If he exhibited sufficiently different behavior, I may not be justified in ascribing a desire, but instead, a belief or some other intentional mode.[22] If there is a change in causal powers, there will be some corresponding change in the principles that justify my ascription of a mental state with a certain intentional mode. Construed this way, (b) does seem to follow from (a); (a)₁: Changes in a state's causal powers in part determine the justification of ascribing a given mental state. Thus, (b)₁: Some differences in causal powers alter whether or not I am justified in ascribing a state with a given intentional mode.

Although this epistemological claim seems more plausible, it does not seem to justify the move from premise two and three to premise four. When a state changes in causal powers, I may not be justified in ascribing the same state to the subject, but that does not entail that the state itself changes in intentional mode. In order for the same state to change in intentional mode, we must know that the same state failed to come to consciousness as the

---

20 John R. Searle "The Connection Principle and the Ontology of the Unconscious: A Reply to Fodor and Lepore," *Philosophy and Phenomenological Research* 54, no. 4 (1994), 853.

21 This seems to be what Crane means when he says attitudes are "functional or dispositional" in relation to one another (cf. Crane 2001, 112).

22 A similar argument could be made for specifically neuropsychological causal powers.

state it is because of a change in causal powers when it became conscious. Thus, Fodor and Lepore need a premise that asserts some metaphysical claim. Namely, if you change the causal powers of a mental state sufficiently, you can change the mental state that it is.

On a second reading of '*determine,*' Fodor and Lepore *are* making this stronger claim. They assert that causal powers in part constitute the very existence of an intentional mode. If you could alter some of the causal powers of a state, you could change the very state that it is. Some of Fodor and Lepore's strong intuitions also support this reading. They assert that "a doubt that P that is functionally indistinguishable from a conviction that P wouldn't *be* a doubt" (841). However, on this reading, it is not as clear how (a₂): Causal powers *in part* determine the very existence of a state with a given intentional mode rather than another, entails (b₂): A change in causal powers can change the very nature of a given mental state.

In fact, it seems clear that this stronger claim (b₂) does not follow. On either reading of "determine", Fodor and Lepore think that intentional modes are functional only "inter alia". That is, intentional modes are not immediately reducible to only the causal powers themselves. Since Fodor and Lepore use the *inter alia* clause in their description of intentional modes, they *are* entitled to the claim that changes in causal powers, in conjunction with other changes in these inter alia attributes of states, supervene on intentional modes. On the epistemological reading of '*determine*', a change in causal powers alone could change whether or not I am justified in ascribing a mental state. However, in terms of the metaphysical reading, a change in causal powers may *never* illicit a change in intentional mode unless it is conjoined with a change in the inter alia facts. This would especially be the case if the inter alia facts actually supervened over the intentional mode facts. Such a thesis would be true on the following model, where the arrows represent a relation of metaphysical supervenience:[23]

Inter alia facts
↓
Intentional mode facts
↓
Causal powers

This model confirms both Fodor and Lepore's intuition and my initial intuition about how causal powers determine intentional modes. First, a state can change its causal powers without a corresponding change in intentional mode. So, when I get tired over the course of the day and a desire loses its causal efficacy, the desire will not become a different attitude. Also, Fodor and Lepore's intuition that "a doubt that P that is functionally indistinguishable from a conviction that P wouldn't *be* a doubt"[24] is also confirmed. Since the intentional mode itself determines the causal powers of a state, a conviction will not be functionally identical to a doubt. Nonetheless, premise two could be false and these intuitions would be wholly confirmed.

Ultimately, premise two loses its plausibility when put forth as a metaphysical thesis. In order to disprove premise two, one would have to give reason to think that a change in causal powers is *never* sufficient for a change in intentional mode. The supervenience model that I give above shows that there are other possible accounts that explain Fodor and Lepore's intuitions. Nonetheless, a decisive negation of premise two would only come from a

---

23 One plausible candidate for the 'inter alia' facts are Searle's "Background" facts (cf. Searle 1992, 175). This model looks consistent with Searle's view.

24 Jerry Fodor, and Ernest Lepore. "What Is the Connection Principle?," *Philosophy and Phenomenological Research* 54, no. 4 (1994): 841.

fully-fledged model of mental causation.

A Misuse of Ontological Identity

Strategy one reveals that Fodor and Lepore must have a way of tracking the ontology of an essentially unconscious state. This comes out in their attempted use of functional powers—they *need* a metaphysical thesis for their argument to work. This is because their objection posits the possibility that a mental state comes to consciousness, as a state with a different intentional mode; that is, it depends on the *same* ontological particular to have a different intentional mode when it becomes conscious. If my analysis is right, Fodor and Lepore are not entitled to the claim that the essentially unconscious state and its conscious correlate are ontologically the same, even when we grant that functional powers determine a mental states' ontology inter alia. I will now suggest that they do not give good reason to think that these two states are ontologically the same.

In order to get clear on the issue here, I want to take a quick deviation and consider an analogy that brings out which facts are unsubstantiated in Fodor and Lepore's objection. Consider a billiard ball factory. Billiard balls are perfectly off-white colored spheres when they are on the conveyor belt just before they get to the stream of red paint that covers them. Just before they get that red coat of paint, however, they are hidden behind a long tube. Now, the pH of the white billiard balls-to-be is constantly regulated. If the pH of the billiard ball is too high, the ball will lose its shape completely and turn into an imperfect sphere. So the billiard comes to the other side of the paint either as a perfect sphere, or an imperfect one depending on the pH of its surface material.

In comparison, an essentially unconscious state is

like a billiard ball with the wrong pH.[25] When it hits the paint, it changes its shape.[26] So, the factory worker (who has extensive knowledge on what sometimes happens in these cases and who can test the pH etc.) has every reason to assume that the same material that was the billiard-ball-to-be is now a misshapen sphere. So she knows that the billiard ball 'came to the other side of the tube' as a misshapen sphere. The point of this analogy is that even though there is a crucial difference in the sphere after it gets painted, the factory worker can track the ontology of the billiard ball; she has every reason to think it is onto-logically identical to the ball that was hidden in the tube just previously, because it is made of the exact same stuff as the other spatio-temporal particular.

Similar to the factory worker's use of 'come to the oth-er side of the tube' Fodor and Lepore seem to have a simi-lar idea of ontology in mind. They seem to presume that an essentially unconscious state is somehow ontologically identical to its token-correlate. We saw that the factory worker can test the pH of the ball and has many ways of measuring if the billiard ball is made of the same stuff as the previous ball behind the tube. However, Fodor and Lepore's conception of "making" an essentially uncon-scious state conscious makes the same inference that the factory worker does without any justification; they give no coherent way of measuring the fact that an uncon-scious state is ontologically identical to its conscious cor-relate.

Unlike the billiard ball factory, there are (at least) two possibilities for the ontology of the essentially uncon-

_____

25 Searle discusses similar analogies that are consistent with our use of 'come to consciousness' like that of "fish in the sea or furniture in the dark attic of the mind" (cf. 1992, 172).

26 And also its functional powers: it can no longer be a used as a bil-liard ball.

scious state. First, it could be that the two states are onto-logically identical, and so it is true that the state *changes* in intentional mode when it becomes conscious. However, there is also another possibility. Namely, the unconscious state could cause a distinct conscious state that bears no relation to the unconscious disposition. These two possi-bilities bring out that Fodor and Lepore give no reason to think that the unconscious state "*changes*" in intentional mode rather than simply *causes* a distinct state with a different intentional mode. There is no reason to think that the essentially unconscious state bears any ontologi-cal relation to the conscious state in this case. Thus, they covertly accept that "making a state conscious" entails having the same ontology, but give no reason to suggest that the state actually does have the same ontology. If this analysis is right, Fodor and Lepore's argument is not only unsound, but invalid.

The Divergence of Ontological and Token-Identity

We saw that Fodor and Lepore's objection covertly as-sumed that two mental states 'come to consciousness' as ontologically identical. Next, I will sketch an argument which states that any view that understands a mental state's ontological identity in terms of its token-identity may fail to understand the ontological difference between conscious episodes and unconscious states. Since uncon-scious belief gives us one type of state that can never be ontologically identical to its conscious correlate, the de-fender of the CP can use belief as a salient example to generate skepticism against the arrival theory. Uncon-scious belief shows that ontological identity and token-identity are entirely distinct in some cases. By showing in one case that there is a distinction between token-identity and ontological identity, then, at the very least, the onus is on the other theorist to demonstrate when (and if ever) token-identity is ontological identity.

Unconscious Belief

Tim Crane argues extensively for the thesis that conscious belief is not ontologically identical to unconscious belief by using the ontological categories mentioned earlier. He writes:

> If a conscious belief were an occurrence, it would exist for as long as that occurrence were to exist. For a belief to cease to be conscious, then, on this understanding, would be for the occurrence to cease, or to go out of existence. But if the occurrence thus went out of existence—for example, when the subject paid attention to something else, or became unconscious—then it cannot play the essential role of belief...So, whatever such an occurrence is, it cannot be belief: "occurrent belief" is not belief at all.[27]

When Crane says that occurrent belief is not belief, he is bringing out the way in which these two states are ontologically distinct. At the unconscious level, belief is a state, while at the conscious level, belief is an event or episode. All the same, unconscious beliefs can be token-identical to conscious beliefs since, as Crane says, they "play the essential role of belief." That is, conscious tokens of an unconscious belief are still endorsements of a given content. So, beliefs can be token-identical even if they fit

27 Tim Crane, "Unconscious Belief and Conscious Thought," in *Phenomenal Intentionality 2013,* ed. Uriah Kriegel (USA: Oxford University Press, 2013), 165.

into different ontological categories.[28] Thus, for belief, it would be a mistake to understand ontological identity as token-identity; unconscious beliefs are token-identical to their conscious correlates but never ontologically identical.[29] Ontologically, unconscious and conscious belief must be distinct, but there is substantial reason to think that these two entities are the *very same* belief.

Now, I want to argue that the defender of the CP can use this analysis of belief to block Fodor and Lepore's objection, and to revise the 'comes to conscious' vocabularies. If this analysis is correct, we could construct the following *reductio ad absurdum*:

1. An arbitrary essentially unconscious could exist, call it S(p), only if ontological identity should be understood to be token-identity (assumption)

2. When S(p) comes to consciousness, it comes to consciousness as $S_2(p)$ (definition of essentially unconscious state)

3. For any token conscious correlate to 'come to consciousness', it must be in some sense ontologically identical to its unconscious state (1, definition of arrival theory)

4. Belief gives us one salient case where a conscious correlate is never ontologically iden-

---

28 Crane considers that the ontology of the brain may be very different to that of the mind, so he seems to think that the distinction between states and events provides only a preliminary account of mental ontology. But it is hard to understand how one can think that these basic ontological categories do not supervene over brain states/events and also be some sort of Realist about intentional states.

29 Interestingly, outside the discussion of the unconscious/conscious distinction, this thesis is identical to 'multiple realization'.

tical to its unconscious disposition (distinction between states and occurrences, Crane's analysis)

5. Ontological identity should not always be understood in terms of token-identity (4)

6. ⊥ : An essentially unconscious state does not exist as outlined in (1) (contradiction: 3,5)[30]

Since an essentially unconscious state requires that some unconscious state's conscious correlate be ontologically identical to it, and since we assert token-identity is not a good guide to ontological identity, we negate (1).

It may be objected that this gives no grounds for thinking that *all* unconscious intentional states are ontologically distinct from their conscious correlates. It is simply a characteristic of belief that unconscious and conscious tokens cannot be ontologically identical. Other intentional states could give us reason to think that there are unconscious episodes that are identical to conscious episodes.[31]

Given our present knowledge of the ontology of the mind, such an objection is entirely warranted. However, I am trying to argue that belief gives us one strong instance where ontological identity could never be explained in terms of token-identity. Of course, it could be that belief

---

30 That is, an essentially unconscious state does not exist on *this* understanding of token-identity and ontological identity. It could be argued that this is the same conclusion of Searle's dispositional account. But, it seems as if this conclusion could be more general. Even on functional characterizations of aspectual shape (contrary to Searle's account) this argument may still go through (for functional characterizations cf. Robert Van Gulick. 206).

31 This seems to require a denial of Searle's Connection Principle.

is not a special case. Belief may be a more salient case of an entirely general phenomenon—unconscious states are *always* ontologically distinct from their conscious correlates. More work is needed to fully substantiate such a claim. However, what *is* established is that unconscious belief can be used argumentatively against Fodor and Lepore to put the burden of substantiating an arrival theory of this unconscious in concrete philosophical terms.

Conclusion

Searle's reply to Freud's question of the ontology of the unconscious gives the unconscious a dispositional form. All unconscious states are dispositions to cause conscious states. Fodor and Lepore then object to the Connection Principle, but their analysis of how causal powers determine intentional modes is not decisive. Further, their argument for the possibility of an essentially unconscious state can be blocked by uncovering hidden ontological assumptions in their argument that appear to come from confusions surrounding our commonsense conception of the unconscious mind. Crane then shows how an assumption of the arrival ontology is not possible for unconscious belief. I suggest that we consider belief a more salient case of a general phenomenon—the full failure of assuming that ontological identity just is token-identity. I take this to show that we need independent notions of token-identity and ontological identity. Consequently, this will require deep revisions of the meaning of "comes to," "arrives in," and "becomes" conscious.

Bibliography

Crane, Tim. *Elements of Mind: An Introduction to the Philosophy of Mind*. U.S.A: Oxford University Press, 2001.

— "Unconscious Belief and Conscious Thought." *Phenomenal Intentionality 2013*, edited by Uriah Kriegel, 156-172. USA: Oxford University Press, 2013.

Fodor, Jerry, and Ernest Lepore. "What is the Connection Principle?." *Philosophy and Phenomenological Research* 54, no. 4 (1994): 837-845.

Freud, Sigmund. "The Unconscious" (1915) reprinted in *Freud: Complete Works*, edited by Ivan Smith, 2011. 2990-3024.

— "Introductory Lectures on Psycho-Analysis" (1916-1917) reprinted in *Freud: Complete Works*, edited by Ivan Smith, 2011. 3124-3501.

Searle, John R. *The Rediscovery of the Mind*. Cambridge: MIT, 1992.

—"The Connection Principle and the Ontology of the Unconscious: A Reply to Fodor and Lepore." *Philosophy and Phenomenological Research* 54, no. 4 (1994): 847-855.

Soteriou, Matthew. "Content and The Stream of Consciousness." *Philosophical Perspectives* 21.1 (2007): 543-68.

Van Gulick, Robert. "Why the Connection Argument Doesn't Work." *Philosophy and Phenomenological Research* 55, no. 5 (1995): 201-207.

Daniel Spina studies philosophy and French at the University of California, Berkeley. He is interested in a wide variety of topics in philosophy of mind, but especially the unconscious. He lives in Oakland, California.

Democracy Promotion as Political Project

Rethinking Democracy as Non-Governmental

Jeta Mulaj
Villanova University, Villanova, USA

Introduction

Democracy is generally understood as an egalitarian constitution of political and social life that encourages citizens to participate in defining their relations, problems, and possibilities. The word democracy, in English, is derived from the Greek word δημοκρατία: the rule of the demos or, more generally, government by the people. Even though democracy was invented in ancient Athens and Rome, it has been continuously reinvented. From antiquity to the present day, different understandings of democracy have produced different political possibilities and goals. While the dominant understanding of democracy has emphasized the rule of the people and shared civic responsibility and power, the fundamental principles of democracy have remained only formally the same. Ancient philosophers such as Plato and Aristotle did not consider democracy to be an ideal form of governance. However, the democracy that Plato and Aristotle criticized only partially resembles today's democratic practices. Today democracy is understood as a form of governance where citizens, through certain political acts such as that of voting, demonstrate their right to elect representatives of the people. This form of democracy is very different from democracy understood as the direct rule of the people.

The contemporary belief in democracy as the one and only ideal form of governance has brought about a new political goal: "democracy promotion." Democracy is viewed as the ideal form of governance which if commenced will bring about democratic social and political relations. Thus, democracy promotion is the attempt of an already established democratic country to institute democracy in so-called underdeveloped countries. While one may be tempted to support such a political project— which seems to aim at creating democratic societies—a closer reading of democracy promotion shows that this project is done for and through undemocratic means. In this paper, I will argue that such promotion is possible only with an understanding of democracy as a particular form of governance, which if applied to a particular society will lead to democratic social and political relations. However, democracy which is not understood as a form of governance, but rather as a form of participation in the political sphere, as a particular way of being a political subject, and as a participation that which critiques state power and opens space for new constitutions of society, and poses limits to the very project of democracy promotion. Drawing on the work of Jacques Rancière, I will argue that a new understanding of democracy that breaks from democracy as a form of governance will set boundaries to the political project of the exportation of democracy.

Plato's Critique of Democracy

Political philosophy has framed democracy in different ways throughout its history. An overview of the different philosophical conceptions of democracy will help us understand how certain framings of democracy open space for various political and social projects, such as democracy exportation. One of the first examples is the Athenian democracy based on debate and civic participation where political knowledge was derived from opinion and action. Ancient philosophers and historians, such as Herodotus, Plato, and Aristotle, were critical of democracy. As a historian with philosophical interests, Herodotus was preoccupied with the problems of the creation of a stable and just city. Examining the characteristics of monarchy, oligarchy, and democracy, he found that the best guarantee of freedom is monarchy where one individual rules according to the laws.[1] Pericles' "Funeral Oration," on the other hand, is a defense of democracy's claim of being the school of civic virtue.[2] Pericles maintained that Athenian democracy was justly administered, as the majority ruled and merit was the criteria for governing the city. Following Herodotus, Plato, and Aristotle were both critics of democracy. In the *Republic*, Plato maintains that in his ideal just city the wise, not the many should rule.[3] Moral and intellectual qualities are rare and transmitted by birth, and this should be the primary factor that defines social status. Heredity principle is crucial to the *polis*, since origin is used to consolidate class distinction and preserve order. Plato's just city is justified

---

1 Philip P. Wiener, *Dictionary of the History of Ideas,* (Charles Scribner's Sons, 1974), Kindle Edition.

2 Wiener. *Dictionary of the History of Ideas.*

3 Alan Bloom, trans., *The Republic of Plato,* (United States: The Perseus Books Group, 1968), (414b8-c1).

on the grounds that one's moral qualities determine one's social role and position. The just city requires that every individual performs the function for which he/she is naturally suited within the social hierarchy. For Plato, political order should be in harmony with the natural order, thus, the foundation for political justice is found in the comparison of harmony of the soul to the just city. The three parts of the city—workers, auxiliaries, and Guardians—by working together and performing their specific role create harmony in the *polis*. Just as the soul is just when appetites and spiritedness are ruled by reason, so the *polis* is just when the philosopher-kings rule the *polis*.

The *polis* derives its wisdom from the Guardians, who are the most fit to rule and who do so through selective lies, myths, and various deceptions.[4] Workers are dominated by their desires and pleasures, thus, they should be ruled by the Guardians.[5] But the *Republic* also operates with a notion of freedom which involves the acceptance of the authority of reason. Freedom is exclusive to those who conceive and comprehend the forms, namely the philosopher-rulers. Few individuals will achieve wisdom, the fundamental virtue that legitimizes power. One of the many anti-democratic elements in Plato's *Republic* is the necessity to possess a certain kind of philosophical knowledge of the Forms to legitimize political participation. Unlike workers who lack virtue, the Guardians in possession of philosophical knowledge are best fit to rule over the rest of society.[6]

Plato does not advocate for a democratic society where the demos rules, but rather a society ruled by the few who possess knowledge: "there will be no end to the

---

4 Bloom, *The Republic*, (428d).

5 Ibid., (590c).

6 Ibid., (432a).

troubles of states…till philosophers become kings in this world, or till those we now call kings and rulers really and truly become philosophers, and political power and philosophy thus come into the same hand."[7] The rule of the Guardians is supported by the ontological transcendence of the forms, for it is essential that the rulers possess qualities that the others lack.[8] Their authoritarian rule becomes justifiable through their exclusive access to an ontological reality. Thus, to challenge the Guardians is to challenge the structure of reality. Given that the workers have, by definition, imbalanced souls, Plato's argument excludes the large majority of citizens from a claim to virtue and political participation. His contempt for the majority extends to their political role, which is the burden of sustaining the other classes who have labor-free ruling positions.[9] The defense of philosophical kingship is itself a repudiation of democracy. Plato argues that chaos is unavoidable without stable standards for the guidance of the *polis,* since democracy honors all pursuits equally and opens the city to disorder. *The Republic*'s conception of justice is a rejection of the democratic belief that citizens have sufficient knowledge to participate in governance. Plato argues that the primary goal of the democratic regime is unrestricted freedom or license to do as one pleases.[10] The main concern regarding democracy is that equals and unequals, those possessing "knowledge" and those with "mere opinions," will be treated equally.[11] Plato maintains that with unrestricted freedom out of democracy arises tyranny.[12]

---

7 Ibid., (473c-d).

8 Ibid., (476b).

9 Ibid., (495b-e; 590c).

10 Ibid., (557b-c).

11 Ibid., (558c).

12 Ibid., (562b-c).

Plato critiques the democratic assumption that all should have the right to participate in politics. He argues that democracy leads to anarchy by giving freedom to everyone to choose their own constitution with no obligation to obey a ruler.[13] Democracy is an anarchic form of society that treats everyone equally: "The extreme of popular liberty is reached…when slaves—male and female—have the same liberty as their owners—not to mention the complete equality and liberty in the relations between the sexes."[14] It destroys the social hierarchy necessary for Plato's *polis*, by obscuring the most essential distinction between free citizens and slaves. If government is a question of knowledge of the Forms then the intellectual abilities of the non-philosophers become the condition for their political participation. He repudiates the principle of the majority, which is the fundamental operating principle of democracy. Insofar as the many are incapable of the right moral behavior they stand in need of political control. Democracy, by definition, must always be government by and for the many. Plato finds democracy inherently unstable, as he excludes the possibility that the *polis* can be just when all citizens participate in governing the *polis*.

Aristotle's Treatment of Democracy

In *Politics,* Aristotle defines democracy as a corrupt regime. Aristotle's *polis* is a city-state, a political association of a multitude of citizens, where one person who is a citizen can only belong to one regime.[15] For Aristotle, the *polis* is defined by the form it takes to reach its *telos*,

---

13 Ibid., (557e-559a).

14 Ibid., (563b).

15 Richard McKeon, *The Basic Works of Aristotle*, (New York: The Modern Library, 2001), (3.1.1275a3-4).

which is understood to be the regime: "it is looking to the regime above all that the *polis* must be said to be the same; the term one calls it can be different or the same no matter whether the same human beings inhabit it or altogether different ones."[16] To understand the *polis,* we need to understand the regime that shapes the *polis.* A *politeia* is "an arrangement of a *polis* with respect to its offices, particularly the one that has authority over all."[17] He argues that the regime is the governing body that has authority in the *polis,* such as the people ruling in a democratic regime.[18] Regimes give form to political communities and each is characterized by a different *telos.* The governing body is the political authority of a *polis.* The correct rule is the rule that holds the common good as the *telos* and does not prioritize the benefit of the ruler. Aristotle differentiates three correct regimes with three corresponding deviations. There are three correct regimes: kinship, the monarchy which is oriented towards the common advantage,[19] aristocracy, the rule by the best, and polity, the regime whose name is common to all regimes when the multitude govern with the interest of the common good. Regarding the deviations, he claims that they are "tyranny from kingship, oligarchy from aristocracy, and democracy from the regime called regime."[20] He claims that "tyranny is monarchy with a view to the advantage of the monarch; oligarchy rules with a view to the advantage of the well-off; democracy rules with a view to the advantage of those who are poor; none of them is with a view to the common good."[21] Democracy seems to be the

---

16 McKeon, *The Basic Works of Aristotle,* (3.3.1276b9-13).

17 Ibid., (3.6.1277b9-10).

18 Ibid., (3.6.1277b10-14).

19 Ibid., (3.7.1279a32-33).

20 Ibid., (3.7.1279b4-5).

21 Ibid., (3.7.1279b5-10).

deviation from the rule of the many. He argues that the action of the democracy "must be admitted to belong to the *polis* in just the same way as the actions of the oligarchy or the tyranny."[22] He claims that democratic regimes do not rule for the common advantage.

Aristotle distinguished between different kinds of democracies. The best form is when the common people are too occupied with their small property to make use of their authority and to hold political assemblies. These citizens are satisfied with electing the rulers and choosing the upper classes for office. Aristotle preferred this to large urban populations who involve themselves in daily management of their affairs, as such, democratic rule opens the way to demagogues and leads to some form of tyranny. This occurs when states are too large, foreign revenue is accessible, and demagogues aggravate the people.[23] All citizens participate in politics, hold office, and use their right to vote. In the assembly, demagogues provoke people to govern. The rich are helpless, have concerns to manage, and lack leisure to attend assemblies. Aristotle is concerned that aristocrats will be outnumbered by the notables and the middle class. The number will make the state disorderly and the notables more oligarchic, leading to instability. The last form of democracy is a kind of fulfillment of democracy. Last democracy is the ultimate form of a degenerate constitution.

For Aristotle, polity—the combination of oligarchy and democracy—is the ideal *polis*. It is dangerous for the stability of the *polis* to have too many rich or too many poor. If oligarchy and democracy are inherently unstable, always tending towards tyranny, then polity promises that moderation as guarantee for stability. However,

22 Ibid., (3.3.1276a14-16).

23 Ibid., (6.1319 b 1-32).

Aristotle does not question slavery. The Greek city-state seemed unimaginable without slavery. He states that slaves would be given freedom only in extreme democracy.

The Reemergence of Democracy in Modernity

Philip P. Wiener, in his article on democracy in the *Dictionary of the History of Ideas,* argues that after Aristotle Rome was characterized by different values even though it continued to rely on Greek thought.[24] The Greek historian Polybius attributed the success of Rome to its mixed constitution, which brought together the consuls of monarchical principle, the aristocratic senate, and the popular democratic assemblies. In checking one another, he believed, they prevented chaos. He wanted to explain the success of the Roman constitution and argue that it would succeed even in different circumstances. Its self-regulating function was its genius: "the three powers are interdependent and each checks and controls the other."[25] Influenced by Polybius, Cicero repeated the conventional taxonomy of states: monarchy, aristocracy, and democracy. He argues that the best state is one that combines the virtues of all three. For the sake of justice, the state should be constituted by the people as an affair of the people. Cicero articulated the possibility of a constitution constructed out of democratic freedom, aristocratic wisdom, and love of the king for the people. Different from Cicero, the stoic philosopher Epictetus suggested that politics is not within the individual's power to change. The wise will not be too concerned with

24 Wiener, *Dictionary of the History of Ideas.*
25 Ibid.

political activities and will not willingly participate. Yet, they will consent to serve the state if asked to do so. This created a different political environment. Wiener argues that there were no novel political institutions or concepts of citizenship to announce. Local rule reasserted itself upon the barbarian invasions and the destruction of Roman authority. In *Dictionary of the History of Ideas,* Wiener states that "even the recovery of Aristotle's writings in the 13th century…did not make the political concerns of the Aegean world altogether meaningful for men who were confronting problems different from those of the Greek city-state."[26] Other historians offered a different viewpoint with the majority agreeing on the importance of the French Revolution.

For new democratic formulations to develop it was necessary for individuals to perceive themselves differently and seek new political participation: "The anxiety that existed in Europe in the 16th and 17th centuries has been frequently remarked on. The disintegration of an earlier religious unity produced a marked disquietude; so, also, did rapid economic changes, with large social dislocations flowing from them."[27] During this time Thomas Hobbes' theories became very compelling. He maintained that the state was created by humans to satisfy their basic needs, and out of the fear that existed due to lack of protection. The state and authority is a human product. Humans, thanks to security provided by a sovereign power, choose to obey. In questioning whether sovereignty should rest with one, a few, or the multitude, he recognized the benefits of monarchy over democracy. Hobbes' contemporaries saw the matter differently, as some expressing a preference for a form of democratic

---

26 Ibid.

27 Ibid.

rule. John Lilburne, leader of the Levellers, argued for the sovereignty of the common people. They demanded universal suffrage, equal electoral districts, biennial parliaments, and sharing of the land.

The philosopher John Locke emerged with a new understanding of political authority. His state of nature, unlike Hobbes, does not start with the assumption of terror and conflict. He believed that reasonable human beings enjoy a form of equality. However, with no common authority to obey, everyone interprets the laws of nature individually. Guided by reason, people join to form societies to escape the state of nature. Through the social contract, individuals give up the right to personally interpret the laws and create a society that guarantees rights of life, liberty, and property. Once the political state is established, authority is fixed within it. Locke believed that the answer to a just rule was offered by democracy.

In the 18th century, the political philosopher Jean Jacques Rousseau argued that awareness of common interests creates a bond between men. These interests arise from a determination to prevent inequality. He argues that the general will expresses the interest that people share. General will imposes justice based on mutual respect and lack of subordination. For Rousseau, the opposite of monarchical subordination is the essence of citizenship. Wiener states that: "What was new, after 1776, and even more after 1789, was not that men could not (or did not) consult the past, but that the more recent past became a more compelling subject of concern to them."[28] Discourse on democracy increased, but it no longer referred back to Greece. The discourse on democracy, no longer referring to the past, began a new stage linked to modern events and to theoretical questions that contem-

28 Ibid.

porary reflections had provoked: "Democracy, a term not much used in the eighteenth century…now came into more general favor, though it was still not employed with the frequency that is sometimes imagined."[29]

An argument can be made that revolutionary democracy reached its peak in 18th century Europe.[30] Rights to liberty, equality, security, and property together with the notion that sovereignty belongs to people as a whole, and that the right to vote should be extended to all males, were constantly being restated. Those who advocated for democracy were characterized by a set of new values. Barely used before the French Revolution, the term democracy by the 19th century had secured both its advocates and enemies.[31] In the 18th century, Jeremy Bentham established his support for universal male suffrage and the secret ballot. He believed that good government originates from the people, that is, in erasing all differences between the interest of the people and those of the government. During the same time, James Mill argued that the middle class should be enfranchised and lead the lower classes with the expectations that they would follow their example. The greatest good of the greatest number of people could result when each individual pursues their own interests. Bentham maintained that if all were permitted to pursue their interests, this would itself provide the check that was needed. The guarantee of good government was the principle of utility.[32]

In the 19th century, John Stuart Mill inquired for a reform of government that would bring the most virtuous individuals in leading positions. Popular govern-

29 Ibid.

30 Ibid.

31 Ibid.

32 Ibid.

ment meant that people are in a position to choose their governors. His philosophy was influenced by Alexis de Tocqueville's *Democracy in America,* an empirical investigation of modern democracy. Tocqueville maintains that the government in America stands in superiority of the majority with the tendency to surpass the limits of its legitimate role. Democracy, he claimed, does not guarantee efficient government. It does provide freedom for the quest of one's interests, but is always subject to the tyranny that leads from the majority insisting that its values should be protected. Tocqueville maintained that equality isolates people, and encourages them to focus on themselves and material goods. Regarding the absolute sovereignty of the majority, he claimed that "it is of the very essence of democratic governments that the empire of the majority is absolute; for in democracies, outside the majority there is nothing that resists it."[33] The interests of the majority are indulged at the expense of the minority. Democracy cannot flourish without equality of conditions and sovereignty of the people. Mill spoke out against the tyranny of public opinion, which he believed should not interfere with individual opinion. The individual is only accountable to society for actions that affect others. For Mill, political responsibility was the greatest good and to be an active political subject must be the goal of everyone capable of doing so. While not everyone directly contributes to politics, all could participate through representative institutions. Ultimately, Mill preferred representative government.

---

33 Alexis de Tocqueville, *Democracy in America*, (Chicago: University of Chicago Press, 2002), 235.

The Collapse of the Classic Paradigm for Democracy

World War I was a significant time for shaping the understanding of democracy.[34] In bringing the U.S into the war in 1917, Woodrow Wilson claimed that he was enrolling the country in a war to make the world safe for democracy. War was meant to guarantee the opportunity for self-government—democracy—to be the prevailing political form of the future: "Democracy became a word of common usage in a way that it had never been previously."[35] Furthermore, during this time, exporting democracy or "democracy promotion abroad" became explicit in U.S politics. Wilson's slogan to end the war and to find a resolution to the turmoil in Europe was to make the world safe for democracy. Exporting democracy became even more explicit during World War II and the Cold War. During the Cold War, common opinion about governance was that the world was divided between democracy, freedom, and capitalism, on one side and communism, socialism, and centralization on the other. The Cold War allowed the rhetoric about democracy promotion to flourish. The U.S. engagement in military intervention now mobilized the rhetoric of democracy promotion.

In the 20th century, there was no possibility in believing, as the 18th century did, that "the democratic method is that institutional arrangement for arriving at political decisions which realizes the common good by making the people itself decide issues through the election of individuals who are to assemble in order to carry out its will."[36] In viewing this as fiction, Joseph Schumpeter argued that the classic democratic theory did not describe

---

34 Wiener, *Dictionary of the History of Ideas.*

35 Ibid.

36 Ibid.

the political situation. He claimed that democracy is the rule of the politician and not of the people. Essential to the persistence of democracy is the agreement of the majority of all classes to accept the rules of the democratic game: '[this] implies that they are substantially agreed on the fundamentals of their institutional structure.'[37]

The Current State of Democracy

Robert Dahl, in *On Democracy*, claims that "during the last half of the 20th century the world witnessed an extraordinary and unprecedented political change. All of the main alternatives to democracy either disappeared, turned into eccentric survivals, or retreated from the field to hunker down in their last strongholds."[38] Anarchy, monarchy, oligarchy, together with communism, lost their validity as opponents of democracy. Today the challenge that nondemocratic countries face is whether and how they can become democratic; a challenge that goes hand in hand with attempts to export democracy. While democracy is not a novel term, the democracy we know today does not resemble the democracy that ancient philosophy was critical of: "Today we have come to assume that democracy must guarantee virtually every adult citizen the right to vote."[39]

While it has become common sense to be a supporter of democracy and to claim that it is the *telos* of today's world, many so-called democratic institutions and goals employ highly undemocratic means to achieve the democratic telos. Alain Badiou, Jacques Rancière, Slavoj Žižek, and Wendy Brown, amongst other contemporary phi-

---

37 Ibid.

38 Ibid.

39 Ibid.

losophers, have expressed their concerns about today's democracy. According to Badiou: "the only way to make truth out of the world we're living in is to dispel the aura of the word democracy and assume the burden of not being a democrat and so being heartily disapproved of by 'everyone' (tout le monde)."[40] Badiou claims that if the democrats' world is not the world in which everyone belongs—if "tout le monde isn't really the whole world after all"[41]—then democracy is just a word for a conservative oligarchy. In the same way that Plato argued that democracy would not save the Greek *polis*, Badiou claims that today's democracy will not save the West. Returning to Plato's critique of democracy, Badiou's critique is aimed at the essence of the democratic state and the constitution of the democratic subject. Resembling Plato's critique of democracy, he maintains that the democratic world is not really a world; the only thing that establishes the democratic subject is pleasure-seeking behavior. Badiou, following Plato's criticism of democracy as a horizon in which everything is equivalent to everything and where truth and opinion are the same, claims that there is a link between democracy and nihilism. Daniel Bensaid claims that Badiou's Platonic critique of democracy reinstates the fear of the tyranny of the number, as the numerical majority is never a proof of justice.[42] In Permanent Scandal, Bensaid states that Rancière draws the contrast between democracy as a permanently extensive moment and democracy as an institution or a regime, which is the understanding of democracy in the common sense. Rancière maintains that democracy is not a form of governance but rather a mode of subjectivation through which

---

40 Agamben et al., "The Democratic Emblem" in *Democracy in What State?* (New York: Columbia University Press, 2011), 7.

41 Ibid.

42 Agamben et al., "Permanent Scandal" in *Democracy in What State?*

political subjects exist. Democracy is an exceptional local and occasional event.

Democracy today, beyond the common agreement that it is the best form of governance, is used for various undemocratic goals such as democracy exportation. Exporting democracy is employed by world powers in underdeveloped, or so-called "third-world countries," with geopolitical interests. How has the understanding of democracy changed to allow for such political projects to take place? How is the concept of democracy resisting challenges and reconfiguration when clear examples of violence posed by democratic pursuits are available? From the notion of democracy as direct participation of people, who come together to discuss the concerns of the day, democracy has come to mean a form of governance that allows citizens to choose their representatives. Democracy today no longer implies the gathering of citizens in making political decisions. Democracy is reduced to democratic procedures within democratic institutions. Democracy is seen as the most fitting form of governance for every nation, since it is believed that it allows human flourishing. Therefore, democracy promotion is often regarded as necessary to ensure world peace and international cooperation. It is believed that democracy, as the best form of governance, can and should be implemented in every nation.

Attempts to export democracy have been a priority of U.S. foreign policy for a long time. Since WWII, U.S. policy elites have maintained that military action has high chances of resulting in successful outcomes wherever used.[43] Rhetoric, economic sanctions, subversion, foreign aid, and military interventions are all means used to

---

43 Daniele Archibugi, "Can Democracy be Exported?" *Widener Law Review* 13 (2006-2007): http://heinonline.org/HOL/Page?handle=hein.journals/wlsj13&div=17&g_sent=1&collection=journals.

export democracy.[44] While many may regard democracy promotion as a selfless humanitarian deed, the undemocratic character of such involvement is often greater than acknowledged. The fundamental problem with democracy promotion is interference with domestic sovereignty and violation of individual rights of the domestic population for self-determination. Democracy promotion is itself a limitation to the creation of a democratic society.

Democracy, not having intrinsic values, is not necessarily always good for everyone. It is the lives that individuals live under democracy that attribute democracy its meaning and purpose. Democracy should not be regarded as an end in itself but, as a means to a better life, in line with the vision created by the domestic population. It should facilitate individuals' quest for better standards of living, better cooperation, and political representation based on consent. According to Jean-Luc Nancy: "democracy means the conditions under which government and organization are de facto possible in the absence of any transcendent regulating principle."[45] Noam Chomsky states, in *Deterring Democracy* that, "It is, after all, hardly a law of nature that a few should command while the multitude obey, that the economy should be geared to ensuring luxuries for some instead of necessities for all."[46] Since democracy is the means to a better life, it must follow that the process that brings about democracy has to conform to the same goal: fostering the quality of life. This is well stated by Sheldon Wolin in *Democracy Incorporated:* "If democracy is about participating

---

44 John M. Owen, "The Foreign Imposition of Domestic Institutions," *The MIT Press* 56 (2002).

45 Agamben et al., "Finite and Infinite Democracy" in *Democracy in What State?*

46 Noam Chomsky, *Deterring Democracy* (New York: Verso, 1991), 109.

in self-government, its first requirement is a supportive culture, a complex of beliefs, values, and practices that nurture equality, cooperation, and freedom."[47] According to Wendy Brown: "no compelling argument can be made that democracy inherently entails representation, constitution, deliberation, participation, free markets, rights, universality, or equality. The term carries a simple and purely political claim that the people rule themselves, that the whole rather than a part of an Other is politically sovereign. In this regard, democracy is an unfinished principle—it specifies neither what powers must be shared among us for the people's rule to be practiced, how this rule is to be organized, nor by which institutions or supplemental conditions it is enabled or secured, features or democracy."[48] The understanding of democracy as something that can be exported and instituted will inevitably lead to violence and will not result in democratic societies.

Exporting Democracy

The understanding of democracy as a form of governance has brought about a political mission of exporting democracy. History contains many instances—such as the recent case of Iraq—where attempts to promote democracy through military action and economic sanctions have led to losses of innocent lives, injuries, and starvation.[49]

---

47 Sheldon Wolin, *Democracy Incorporated* (Princeton: Princeton University Press, 2008), 260-261.

48 Agamben et al., "We Are All Democrats Now" in *Democracy in What State?* 45-46.

49 Denis J.Halliday, "The Deadly and Illegal Consequences of Economic Sanctions on the People of Iraq," The Brown Journal of World Affairs VII, no.1 (2002), http://www.watsoninstitute.org/bjwa/archive/7.1/Essays/Halliday.pdf.

In Iraq, during the sanctions' regime, severe conditions resulting from sanctions led to the death of 1.5 million people.[50] Human suffering becomes a means to achieve democracy. Iraq is one of the many examples that make visible the violent and non-democratic features of democracy promotion.

Democracy will flourish only if the norms, culture, tradition, and the mechanism of individual cooperation of a society fit with the system: "It [rapid change] is a "reality" constructed from decisions arrived at within a certain framework—itself not accidental."[51] Wolin calls this *the political economy of change*. Rapid change is not a neutral force that exists independently of will, action, considerations of power, comparative advantage, and ideological biases. For democracy to reflect the will and culture of individuals, it must emerge from an uninterrupted filtration of social and political norms. This process of filtration can take time—as norms compete, get accepted, rejected, transfigured, and replaced over time. This competition among social, political, and economic norms leads to a political system that—even if not democracy—represents the will of the people. Wendy Brown states that: "Democracy, rule by the people, is only meaningful and exercisable in a discreet and bounded entity—this is what sovereignty signals in the equation of popular sovereignty with democracy."[52] For people to rule themselves there must be a recognizable collective body within which the sharing of power is organized and upon which it is exercised.

Democracy promotion is a politics of the powerful.

---

50 Gordon, Joy. *Invisible War: The United States and the Iraq Sanctions.* Cambridge (Mass.): Harvard UP, 2010. Print.

51 Wolin, *Democracy Incorporated*, 275.

52 Agamben et al., "We Are All Democrats Now..." in *Democracy in What State?* 49.

There has never been a case when a weaker country imposed institutions or ideals on a stronger country. As Archibugi states, "You cannot impose if you do not have the power to do so."[53] Exporting democracy has been a priority for many powerful countries. This power imbalance must encourage us to scrutinize the commonly asserted reasons for democracy promotions such as world peace and security. According to Chomsky, the thesis of seeing American-style democracy duplicated in the world is not commonly expressed, or argued over, being simply presupposed as the basis for a reasonable discourse on the role of the U.S. in the world.

Forcible promotion occurs when powerful countries expand their power. Moreover, instances of democracy promotion happen when powerful countries bring targeted countries under their influence, usually by imposing political institutions that are most prone to keeping their ideologies in power.[54] Democracy promotion presents the opportunity to augment the imbalance of power in favor of the powerful, and allows them to gain influence over many smaller countries. Exporters of democracy regard other democratic regimes as better trading partners, less prone to war, and more supportive allies when it comes to international disputes.[55] It has often been the case that the targeted countries have had some geopolitical importance for the exporting country either for military or trading purposes.[56] Natural resources have also been a major reason for democracy promotion. Many institutional promotions were imposed on the oil-rich

---

53 Archibugi, "Can Democracy be Exported?"
54 Owen, "Foreign Imposition of Domestic Institutions."
55 Archibugi, "Can Democracy be Exported?"
56 Owen, "The Foreign Imposition of Domestic Institutions."

Middle East due to its abundance of natural resources.[57] Furthermore, the targeted country can become vital for the exporting country if the exporter's rival has already established some importance on the target country.[58]

Exporting democracy means imposing a new regime on a subjected country. While democracy promotion rhetoric suggests that exporting democracy is advantageous for the occupied population, every population desires to participate in the governance of their country. Archibugi asserts that: "Anyone wishing to export democracy must therefore be sure that their intervention will be appreciated and not perceived by the population as merely the replacement of one internal authoritarian regime with another imposed from the outside."[59] Since powerful countries usually impose their institutions on target countries, the local population has not necessarily consented to that type of governance. Moreover, considering that many democracy promotion attempts have led to local economic destruction due to military interventions, deaths of many individuals due to the shortages of food resulting from economic sanctions, and starvation due to military action and sanctions, the local population is often prone to resisting the new administration.

External interference leads to the "rally-around-the-flag" effect, despite the fact that the domestic population may be living under a dictator.[60] The population of an occupied country becomes aggressive when they confront the administration installed by the exporter. This aggression can become perpetual with long lasting consequences and it is a response to the fact that the installed

---

57 Ibid.

58 Ibid.

59 Archibugi, "Can Democracy be Exported?"

60 Ibid.

administrations have almost no contact with the local population. In Afghanistan and in Iraq, the installed administrations have little or no affinity with the populations, often leading to major hostilities.[61] During the economic sanctions regime, 1991 – 2003, Iraqis blamed United States for all of their economic destitution. Instead of going against their totalitarian leadership – what United States aimed for – their political integration instead became a support for Saddam's regime.

Exporting democracy is anti-democratic. It is perceived as "the right thing to do" to help those suffering under repressive and brutal regimes. Western guilt ignores the mechanisms of foreign policy goals and focuses on intentions. Regardless of the intentions, there are two major anti-democratic characteristics of the attempts to export democracy, which defeat the purpose of intervention itself. First, exporting countries promote their own institutions.[62] Intervening in order to overthrow an existing government and install a new one that conforms to its interests is undemocratic. Interventions of this nature ignore the freedom of people to choose their form of governance. Second, mechanisms of democracy promotion have led to losses of lives, injuries, and starvation, such as the recent examples of the victims of economic sanctions in Iraq and Iran. If exporting democracy is meant to help those under non-democratic regimes, then the exporting country should not regard lost lives as "collateral damage." Archibugi best explains this, when he states that: "In the moment in which one opts to use military force to promote democracy, there arises a contradiction between the means and the ends. The violent means of war do not exclusively involve despots, but they inevitably end up

---

61 Ibid.

62 Owen, "Foreign Imposition of Domestic Institutions."

also having an impact on the citizens, whom we assume would benefit from a democratic regime. Despite surgical bombardments, smart bombs, and other technological developments, war is still a dirty affair, with consequences that impact entire populations indiscriminately."[63]

Another anti-democratic feature of democracy promotion is the fact that the politics of such promotion equate people with their government. When a foreign policy is imposed on a certain country, it is the domestic population, not the political leaders, who bear the costs. Usually the domestic population is assumed to be the best means to reach out to the leadership and influence policy. Equating people with their governments is analogous to punishing them for things they have not done, since the interests of the government and the interests of the people in today's democratic societies are entirely separate.

For social norms to persist they must emerge from within. Social and political norms have to go through the process of peaceful competition and filtration, during which some norms are accepted, some rejected, some transfigured, and some replaced. This process ensures that norms are well suited for the population of that country. Many attempts of the U.S to promote democracy have failed in places such as Haiti, Panama, Nicaragua, Dominican Republic, and Cuba.[64] Moreover, the attempts of the U.S. to export democracy failed for three decades in South Korea.[65] After WWII, only Panama and Grenada were considered successful interventions.[66] Bosnia and Kosova, the more recent interventions, are still considered unsuccessful in terms of exporting democra-

---

63 Archibugi, "Can Democracy be Exported?"

64 Ibid.

65 Ibid.

66 Ibid.

cy.[67] And the most recent examples, military intervention in Iraq and Afghanistan, help further argue about the failures of such attempts.[68] Democracy promotion has become a tool to promote institutions and ideologies that conform to the exporter's interests. While many still regard the exporter's attempts for democracy promotion as means to a "stable, legitimate, and prosperous international order,"[69] it is evident that world stability and peace are not exporter's main objective. A great example is the U.S, which – while it claims to be concerned with world's peace and stability – has spent decades in supporting dictatorial regimes or overthrowing democratically elected governments.[70]

The dominant discourse today perceives democracy as a form of government to be the answer to all international disputes, despite the fact that the mechanism of implementation and those making decisions can significantly impact the manifestation of democracy. While today the institution to be promoted is democracy, the desired institutions to be promoted can change depending on the geopolitics of the powerful. Thus the question that follows is: what understanding of democracy allows for such pursuits or goals? Different moments in history have presented different understanding of what democracy is and as a result they have manifested different opportunities, possibilities, and ends to achieve. The way in which democracy is understood leads to various ways of under-

---

67 Ibid.

68 Ibid.

69 G. John Ikenberry, "Why Export Democracy?" The Wilson Quarterly 23, No.2 (1999). http://www.jstor.org/stable/pdfplus/40259885.pdf?acceptTC=true.

70 Justin Elliot, "What Other Dictators Does the U.S. Support?" *Salon.* February 2, 2011. http://www.salon.com/2011/02/02/american_allies_dictators/.

standing social and political life and civic participation. What kind of understanding of democracy is required for politics of exporting democracy to take place?

Exporting democracy is one example of politics today based on undemocratic means. However, there have been other examples in history where democracy has relied on forms of exclusion and other undemocratic features. Athenian democracy excluded the majority of the population—women, slaves, foreigners, and children—from political participation. As Wendy Brown states: "Democracy as concept and practice has always been limned by a nondemocratic periphery and unincorporated substrate that once materially sustains the democracy and against which it defines itself."[71] Historically, all democracies as we know them today have functioned on the basis of undemocratic features. Brown believes that what powers must be governed and what people must legislate together are not implicated in the definition of democracy. Brown maintains that "we would have to seek knowledge and control of the multiple forces that construct us as subjects, produce the norms through which we conceive reality and deliberate about the good, and present the choice we face when voting or even legislating."[72] For democracy to be meaningful it must reach the fabrics of power that have not been touched previously. She maintains that democracy is an unreachable goal but at the same time a continuous political project of the people. This way of understanding democracy goes beyond a definition of democracy as a form of governance and even further from representative democracy.

---

71 Agamben et al., "We Are All Democrats Now…" in *Democracy in What State?*, 51.

72 Agamben et al., "We Are All Democrats Now…" in *Democracy in What State?*, 53.

The Future of Democracy

Contemporary philosophical work on democracy, such as the work of Rancière, Wolin, and Brown, alter the dominant understanding of democracy as a form of governance. Current discourse on democracy is an invitation to rethink democracy in a way that reconstitutes the democratic horizon to allow for people to determine the freedom of their action. Can democracy be thought of as a way of shaping social and political relations? Can democracy be understood as a form of communicating, instituting and challenging norms, and as a way of political participation, which exceeds governmental forms? If so, what are the implications of such understanding of democracy and how does this limit the politics of democracy promotion? Democratic countries today need the nondemocratic countries—the other—in order to legitimize their power while also constantly trying to appropriate the other according to specific values and ideologies. A new way of understanding democracy can change this relationship between democratic formal governments and underdeveloped undemocratic countries. So far, democracy has been understood as a form of governance which can be applied to, and instituted in, any given country. Yet, attempts to institute democracy have shown that democracy promotion as a political project, based on an understanding of democracy as a form of governance, does not lead to democracy but to violence.

Wolin's premise is that democracy has to be reconceived as something other than a form of government. Wolin does not believe in the idea that democracy can be achieved as a form of government with a particular set of political arrangements and a specific pattern of political relations. Democracy in the modern age is not institutionalizable. For there to be democracy it has to be a moment that challenges the established order and suspends it for a while. Understanding democracy not as a form of government suggests that the political constitutes itself internally: "as a will toward commonality within the ranks of those who experience injustice...self-creating of the demos."[73] Wolin, in *Fugitive Democracy, Difference and Recognition,* maintains that ordinary citizens are capable of creating new cultural patterns at any moment.[74] While everyone has this capability he does maintain that there have to be particular conditions in place for this to occur. Along with other contemporary thinkers, Rancière and Wolin invite us to go beyond an understanding of democracy as simply a form that can be applied to a given state. According to Rancière: "Democracy, in the sense of the power of the people, the power of those who have no special entitlement to exercise power, is the very basis of what makes politics thinkable. If power is allotted to the wisest or the strongest or the richest, then it is no longer politics we are talking about."[75] These new formulations of democracy not only break with the repressive limitations of representative versus direct democracy; they restrict the promotion of democracy that is based on the idea that it is possible to implement democracy in any specific country given that it is a form of governance.

Rancière maintains that democracy should not be conceptualized as a governmental regime, but as the establishment of political subjects through a manifesta-

73 Wiener, *Dictionary of the History of Ideas.*

74 Aryeh Botwinick and William E. Connolly, *Democracy and Vision: Sheldon Wolin and the Vicissitudes of the Political,* (New Jersey: Princeton University Press, 2001).

75 Agamben et al., "Democracies Against Democracy" in *Democracy in What State?,* 79.

tion and demonstration of injustice or "a wrong."[76] Thus, democracy regards the power of those who do not have power, the power of those who are not qualified for governmental order, and the power of those who do not have what it takes to partake in the social order. When this body of unqualified citizens intervenes they install a dissensus; this body demonstrates that they are equal in the intervention and that they are capable of participating in what they have been excluded from. For Rancière, this is the reason why democracy is feared and even hated. The incompetent body of citizens demonstrating their equality is threatening. As we have seen in the ancient world with Plato's ethics, a link between having power and having particular qualifications is reinforced today. The question of democracy for Rancière, the question regarding its meaning, is crucial for it is about the capacity of whoever to speak and to act. The power of the demos, demonstrated in dissensus, is not the power of the majority in the traditional sense of the term. It is the power and the capacity of the whoever. Dissensus is what Rancière identifies as the expression of the political that challenges the dominant order and thus is the space where democracy emerges. Democracy cannot be planned or institutionalized. Democracy is the actual which shifts the field of possibilities.

Politics itself, for Rancière, enacts dissensus. As Samuel A. Chambers states *in Lesson of Ranciere*: "This means that politics comes but seldom, and only by way of a never predictable, and always insurrectionary, moment. This is a moment when a given order of domination and a given regime of hierarchy are radically called into question

---

76 Paul Bowman and Richard Stamp, *Critical Dissensus: Reading Ranciere*, (New York: Continuum International Publishing Group, 2011).

by the emergency of a political subject, a demos."[77] The demos does not exist prior to the appearance on the political. The participation in politics makes the democratic subject, which declares "a wrong," and in doing so brings about politics.[78] Thus, politics is not an act synchronous with the governmental order, such as the right to vote. Politics is always an interruption and an intervention for the sake of disrupting what is. As Chambers states in *The Lessons of Rancière*, if democracy is not a form of government, we cannot live in it.[79]

Speaking about the troubling expression of democracy, Rancière states that democratic societies, with the aim of equality for everyone, are threatening: "the thesis of the new hatred of democracy can be succinctly put: there is only one good democracy, the one that represses the catastrophe of democratic civilization."[80] He claims that today democracy triumphs when the practical benefits are separated from the utopia of the government of the people by the people. "Bringing democracy to another people does not simply mean bringing it the beneficial effects of a constitutional state, elections and free press. It also means bringing disorder."[81] Today a good government is the government capable of controlling the evil called democracy. Hatred for democracy, he claims, is provoked by the intensity of democracy or the actualization of democratic life. This is because democratic life seems to have an anarchic principle which affirms the

<hr>

77 Samuel A. Chambers, *The Lessons of Rancière*, (Oxford University Press, 2013), 8.

78 Chambers, *The Lessons of Rancière*, 16.

79 Ibid., 887.

80 Jacques Ranciere, *Hatred of Democracy*, (New York and London: Verso, 2009), 4.

81 Ranciere, *Hatred of Democracy*, 5-6.

power of the demos.[82] For Rancière, confronting democratic vitality today takes the form of a double bind. Either democracy implies the participation of a large population in the discussion of public affairs, which is not a
good thing, or it stand for a form of social life that focuses on individual satisfaction, which is also not a good
thing. Thus, good democracy is the form of governmental
life that controls the double excess of collective activity
and individual withdrawal inherent to democracy.[83] Yet,
Rancière does not believe that democracy is inapplicable
to today's world. Democracy, as understood by Rancière,
disrupts the social order and the social relations. Democracy inverts the relation of the governing and the governed, and in the same fashion it inverts all other relations.[84]

Rancière understands democracy as an anarchic
'government', based on the absence of every title to govern.[85] So far we have been governed by those who hold
a title to govern us. Rancière maintains that in history
we have known two forms of governing entitlements: the
superiority of birth and the power of wealth. "If the el-
ders must govern not only the young but the learned and
the ignorant as well, if the learned must govern not only
the ignorant but also the rich and the poor, if they must
compel the obedience of the custodians of power and be
understood by the ignorant, something extra is needed,
a supplementary title, one common to those who possess all these titles but also to those who do not possess
them."[86] The remaining title is the anarchic one. This is

---

82 Ibid., 7.

83 Ibid., 8.

84 Ibid., 38.

85 Ibid., 41.

86 Ibid., 46.

democracy—neither a constitution nor a form of society. The power of the people is the power peculiar to those who have no more entitlements to govern than to submit. This power is apolitical power which signifies the power of those who have no natural reason to govern over those who have no natural reason to be governed. The power of the people, of anyone at all, is the equality of capabilities to occupy the positions of governors and of the governed. Political government, then, has a foundation, which for Rancière is a contradiction: "politics is the foundation of a power to govern in the absence of foundation."[87] Democracy, thus, is the challenging of government and the movement that displaces the limits of the public and the private, of the political and the social.[88]

Democracy interrupts: "the timeless logic according to which societies are governed by those who have a title to exercise their authority over those who are predisposed to submit to it."[89] Rancière emphasizes the fact that democracy is not to be understood as either a form of society or a form of government. Societies today that call themselves democratic are a play of oligarchies. He maintains that there is no such thing as a democratic government since government necessarily implies the exercise of the minority. He does not want to associate democracy with a juridico-political form. The power of the people, he claims, is always either beneath or beyond these forms. Rancière maintains that the practice of any form of government shrinks he public sphere and makes it its own private sphere. Thus, democracy struggles against the privatization of the public sphere for the sake of enlarg-

---

87 Ibid., 49.

88 Ibid., 71.

89 Ibid., 51.

ing it.[90]

An understanding of democracy that follows the foot-steps of Rancière's thought in not reducing democracy to a form of government, limits democracy promotion. Democracy as a form of government—in today's world as the ideal form of government—is thought of as a form that can be applied to any given state and which as a result of certain procedures will develop a democratic state, procedure, and relations. It follows that one can foster democracy beyond one's own physical borders. However, an understanding of democracy, as Rancière and Wolin suggest, as a mode of political and social relations, a space in which political subjects are allowed and encouraged to participate, limits the possibilities of exporting democracy. Democracy as the political act which suspends that which is, which challenges the dominant governmental order, and democracy which gives a voice to those who were not qualified to partake in the political, does not allow for democratic promotion which imposes institutions in a people. As Wolin maintains, for democracy to flourish and manifest the norms, the culture, the tradition, and the relations of individuals it must emerge from an uninterrupted competition of social and political norms. Moreover, as Brown states: "Democracy, rule by the people, is only meaningful and exercisable in a discreet and bounded entity—this is what sovereignty signals in the equation of popular sovereignty with democracy. Democracy detached from a bounded sovereignty jurisdiction (whether virtual or literal) is politically meaningless: for the people to rule themselves, there must be an identifiable collective entity within which their power sharing is organized and upon which it is exercised."[91] Democracy

---

90 Ibid., 54-55.

91 Agamben et al., "We Are All Democrats Now..." in *Democracy in What State?*, 49.

is neither a society to be governed nor a government of a particular society. As Rancière maintains, it is "specifically this ungovernable on which every government must ultimately find out it is based."[92]

The notion of democracy has experienced many alternations. Democracy critiqued by Plato and Aristotle was understood as a direct involvement of the demos in articulating and discussing the issues of the day. The democracy that has developed today is one which allows for citizens to choose the minority by which they want to be represented. Representative democracy is reduced to governmental procedures. This formulation of democracy has brought about democracy promotion as a political project of the powerful. Since different understandings of democracy have produced different possibilities and political projects, a reconstitution of democracy may be the solution to ending democracy promotion.

Bibliography

Agamben et al. *Democracy in What State?* New York: Columbia University Press, 2011.

Archibugi, Daniel, "Can Democracy be Exported?" *Widener Law Review* 13 (2006-2007).

Bates, Angell Clifford. *Aristotle's "Best Regime:" Kingship, Democracy, and the Rule of Law.* Louisiana: Louisiana State University Press, 2003.

Bloom, Alan, trans. *The Republic of Plato.* United States: The Perseus Books Group, 1968.

Botwinick, Aryeh, and Willim E. Connolly. *Democracy and Vision: Sheldon Wolin and the Vicissitudes of the Political.* New Jersey: Princeton University Press, 2001.

Bowman, Paul, and Richard Stamp. *Critical Dissensus: Reading Rancière.* New York: Continuum International Publishing Group, 2011.

Chambers, Samual A. *The Lessons of Ranciere.* Oxford University Press, 2013.

92 Rancière, *Hatred of Democracy,* 49.

Chomsky, Noam. *Deterring Democracy*. New York: Verso, 1991.

Day, James, and Chambers, Mortimer. *Aristotle's History of Athenian Democracy*. Berkeley and Los Angeles: University of California Press, 1962.

Elliot, Justin. "What Other Dictators Does the U.S. Support?" *Salon*. February 2, 2011. http://www.salon.com/02american_allies_dictators.

Finley, M.I. *Democracy Ancient and Modern*. New Jersey: Rutgers University Press, 1973,

Gordon, Joy. *Invisible War: The United States and the Iraq Sanctions*. Cambridge (Mass.): Harvard UP, 2010.

Halliday, Denis D, "The Deadly and Illegal Consequences of Economic Sanctions on the People of Iraq," *The Brown Journal of World Affairs* VII, no.1 (2002).

Ikenberry, John G. "Why Export Democracy?" *The Wilson Quarterly* 23, No.2 (1999).

Kraut, Richard, and Skultety, Steven. *Aristotle's Politics: Critical Essays*. Rowman & Littlefield Publishers, Inc., 2005.

McKeon, Richard. *The Basic Works of Aristotle*. New York: The Modern Library, 2001.

Owen, John M, "The Foreign Imposition of Domestic Institutions," *The MIT Press* 56 (2002).

Rancière, Jacques. *Hatred of Democracy*. New York and London: Verso, 2009.

Samaras, Thanassis. *Plato on Democracy*. New York: Peter Lang Publishing, Inc., 2002.

Tocqueville, Alexis de. *Democracy in America*. Chicago: University of Chicago Press, 2002.

Wiener, Philip P. *Dictionary of the History of Ideas*. Charles Scribner's Sons, 1974. Kindle Edition.

Wolin, Sheldon. *Democracy Incorporated*. New Jersey: Princeton University Press, 2008.

Jeta Mulaj is a Kosovar student completing her undergraduate degree in philosophy and honors at Villanova University. Her research interests include political philosophy, psychoanalysis, critical theory, and art. Her interest in philosophy is embedded in her cultural experience in Kosova, leading her to conduct research on revolutions, democracy, mass mobilization, political efficacy, and violence. Besides conducting research in the field of philosophy, she is also an active member of the Marx Reading Group in Kosova, the Anthropological Association of Theory and Praxis, Phi Sigma Tau, and the Kosovar movement for self-determination (VETEVENDOSJE!).

The Taboo of Touch

Alexandra Bischoff
Emily Carr University, Vancouver, Canada

Beginning of Being: Benign in Bed
(An Anecdote)

I am a decapitated form, swimming through a swarthy sea of blankets. An itch calls my fingers forth; I touch my body as if for the first time, and am shocked by the desire to share such a small, forgotten portion of my person. To touch is to know, to touch is to see. Now I want to see others in the same fullness—even if only by touching a fraction of their skin. Thus, the following exercise was born.

(First, a disclaimer: Touching does not require saturated sexuality. Under what circumstances with which we touch is entirely interpretable, and consent is of the highest import.)

The Touching Game

(All that is necessary are two willing participants, and a few minutes of time.)

Spend the first 90 seconds searching your own form for a crook, plane or division of skin. Pay close attention to the sensitivity of this search: are you looking in all the obvious places? Are you sifting above or below layers of cloth? Does touching require the hand to shape around it, or do you use only the fingertips? Is this spot suitable to share with the person beside you?

Next, both give and take clear instructions on how to touch. Spend the next 30 seconds (at least) to share this newfound portion of person with your partner. Do not become overwhelmed by the alien nature: touching with purpose produces results. Resist the urge to move your hand away from the instructed location. Try to trust this touch like it was still your own. You are fleshier than you remember. So are they. The thought of this makes me want to eat a piece of cake.

Embedded Touch

The restrictive-commodification of touch stimulates my desire, especially through artwork. The touching taboo in museum or gallery culture is sternly enforced by velvet ropes or nylon belts, which I might touch instead (if only for compensation). I would argue: an individual can only become personal with a work when close proximity is offered. I can only imagine how personable a painting might become, if trembling tips of fingers felt the furrowed surface. But I am ahead of myself; the desire to touch is impulsive and elusive. If I want to touch, I need to know both the history of touching and my own motivations for touching.

Touch can contemporarily be understood with extreme precision. Paul Thomas uses an Atomic Force Microscope in his 2009 project *Midas,* in order to explore the cell transference of touching gold at the nano level.[1] As an artist, Thomas is committed to studying the advancements of nanotechnology, because they "[force] us to rethink the way that we comprehend and engage with the material world".[2] This nano-level-perspective offers visibility to the invisible through touch.

I am especially interested in how this corroborates animistic intuitions, because at "an atomic level, the body may be envisaged as having no spatial boundaries" at all.[3] Or put in another way, we embed ourselves in what we touch. Thomas quotes Boccioni's *Technical Manifesto of Futurist Painting* in order to illustrate this understanding: "Our bodies penetrate thesofas upon which we sit, and the sofas penetrate our bodies".[4] Perhaps this explains why we desire so greatly to touch an artwork: so that we might become a part of it.

These are the facts of touch, but I want to work from taboo. Touch has complicit societal restrictions; when and why do we touch, and where does touch overlap with art?

Touch-Screens as Teleprompters

It will be beneficial to work backwards, beginning with our most modern form of touch: the back- lit screen. Technology requires touch more than any other medium, because machines are incapable of operating

---

1 Paul Thomas, "Midas: A Nanotechnological Exploration of Touch," *Leonardo* 42.4, (2009), 186.

2 Ibid.

3 Ibid.

4 Ibid., 187.

without it. Doug Back comments that these interactive systems spend most of their time idly, simply "waiting for a person to do something".[5] But these technological devices do not encourage sensitivity from our human forms. Far from being an organic interaction, we can watch any user become as stiff as their devices, while attentions glean the backlit screen.

Vancouver sculpture and media artist Daniel Jolliffe is interested in exploiting these stiffened interactions. In *Room for Walking* (1999), Jolliffe offers an image which can only be fully seen if the participant is willing to vigorously engage with the sculpture. By pushing a heavy wagon around the gallery space, a screen will slowly reveal more of the image. Another work, *Untitled Ball* (1992-93), is strictly evasive, utilizing motion sensor technology so that a large wooden ball will continuously roll away from an approaching viewer.[6]

Room for Walking makes our usually consolidated technological-touch into a physical struggle; *Untitled Ball* denies our desire to touch, while still amplifying technologies' requirement for human movement to make decisions. In either example however, touch is explored primarily as the means, not the incentive. Here, the reward of touching or attempting to touch is still visually embodied. This might be because touch and technology is a numbing combination. There is no tactility to a screen, or to moulded plastic. Numbed-touch does not teach me anything about the physical world. I want to touch a painting for the sake of revelling in the connection between flesh and flesh.

---

5 Doug Back, "Interactivity: (to Act on One Another)," *Touch: Touché : An Exhibition of Interactive Works*, comp. Nina Czegledy, (Toronto: InterAccess Electronic Media Arts Centre, 1999), 13.

6 Ibid., 9.

Decomposition

As delicious as touching can sound, I cannot escape the reasons why touching a painting is faux pas. They destroy the surface—those oily skin cells, embedding themselves into the deliberate and virgin surface. Paintings are romantically regarded as eternal. But the survivability of art objects in general, is not always of main concern to an artist. The passage of time, as is focused upon in performance art, can become the defining nature of an art object.

In a 1999 interview, performance artist Marina Abramovich meditates on the temporality of the art object. She protests the romantic ideal of forever-lasting objects, and instead proclaims that the objects in her audience-participation pieces "[should] be used and, by use, destroyed".[7]

She goes on to explain that this invokes discovery of our own bodily temporalities, through aging.[8] What is particularly relieving regarding this approach is a conscious release from the static and "imperishable" status of an artwork. We could consider it as therapy toward a sense of our own mortality.

And why shouldn't a painting die? It is a great gift to the future to preserve a painting, but there are already so many paintings, so many gestures of preservation. More than for the moral obligation to protect, we inject our own fragile egos into the work because it will outlast us—so long as nobody touches it.

---

7 Janet A. Kaplan, "Deeper and Deeper: Interview with Marina Abromovic," *Art Journal Summer* 58.2, (1999), 10.

8 Ibid.

Touching on the Ego

No one but the reputable restoration specialist has ever been welcomed to touch. Agnes Gertrude Richards writes about the role of this specialized touch, in her 1915 article "The Romance of Restoring". She espouses that every trade has "its secrets and...elements of romance. Occupations touching art at any point are never without this fascination and that of restoring old pictures is particularly rich in romantic interests".[9] This romanticism evolves out of ritual; a precision re-enactment of an artist's creative decisions has never been more palpable than through the restorers touch. Restorers must play detective and become keenly observant to materials and layers, in order to not disturb the surface. Richard explains that even simply cleaning a painting can be tricky, because there are "pictures from which the varnish cannot be removed as the colors themselves have been glazed in with the varnish".[10] Thus, this touching must be sensitive to the needs of the material. And sensitive touch may reveal great secrets; "the discovery of a rare old picture hidden beneath the varnish of a former repair" is a privilege of the restoration trade.[11]

> We do revere the old, even if only for their physical representation of the intangible passage of time. The restorer also teaches us that the aging process cannot and should not be entirely removed—part of why we want to touch is because we can see authenticity in the spreading cracks. But I still think that *all paintings want to be*

9 Agnes Gertrude Richards, "The Romance of Restoring." *Fine Arts Journal* Nov. 33.5, (1915), unnumbered.

10 Ibid.

11 Ibid.

touched—respectively, responsively, retroactively, responsibly. *Intimately.*

;*Look ;Closely ;Touch ;Gently*

The painting touches itself, touches the wall, touches our eyes. It is true that touching is almost synonymous to looking; that we caress objects with our vision. This non-physical touch is fruitful, but there are understandings of self that cannot be achieved without a more literal feeling. Even though touching is an exploration of another body, our findings are always informed in relation to the self. What can a painting learn about itself, while touching sterile gallery walls?

The painting will still *speak* to us, even if we do not touch it. This is why the unaddressed question of touch seems unimportant: *speech* does not seem at first to be physical. However, Jean-Louis Chrétien says that "[there] is no voice but the bodily voice: our whole body is thus presupposed by voice, required in order for voice to be a voice in the first place, and voice in turn transforms the body into a word-bearer".[12] In this sense, we can consider all paintings to be bodily-manifestations of voice, although a voice unconscious of itself because of its physical isolation from the world.

Along with being denied the intimate touch of its viewers, the painting has been denied Lacan's metaphysical mirror. It will not know itself. It will only perpetually repeat its programmed speech. What could a painting teach us if it were gifted the capacity for self-reflection? Could we enter into a more complex and

---

12 Jean-Louis Chrétien, "Body and Touch." *The Call and the Response*, trans. Anne A. Davenport, (New York: Fordham UP, 2004), 85.

extended dialogue with a painting, if we were able to hold it?

In a technological age, where touch is becoming increasingly insensitive, the raw tactility of paint is therapeutic and instinctually-grounding. The sensuous materiality of paint is unlike any other art-flesh; it almost quivers with potentials for touch. But the touching taboo compels distance between the pulse of blood and the pulse of pigment, and I do not see the validity in such an enforced estrangement. Preservation seems a noble task, but once unmasked, these protective gestures read more as egotism than gallantry. And in fact, we stand to learn more about ourselves, more about the speech of a painting, more about the process of death, when touching is an option. Often we back away from a painting in order to gain greater visual perspective. But if we closed that gap and became practitioners of a sensitive touch, we would become more sensitive in sight as well.

Bibliography

Back, Doug. "Interactivity: (to Act on One Another)." *In Touch, Touché: An Exhibition of Interactive Works*, 13-16. Edited by Nina Czegledy. Toronto: InterAccess Electronic Media Arts Centre, 1999.

Chrétien, Jean-Louis. "Body and Touch." In *The Call and the Response*, 83-133. Translated by Anne A. Davenport. New York: Fordham UP, 2004.

Jollifee, Daniel. "Room for Walking: Daniel Jolliffe." *In Touch, Touché: An Exhibition of Interactive Works*, 8-9. Edited by Nina Czegledy. Toronto: InterAccess Electronic Media Arts Centre, 1999.

Kaplan, Janet A. "Deeper and Deeper: Interview with Marina Abromovic." *Art Journal* 58, no. 2 (1999): 6-21.

Richards, Agnes Gertrude. "The Romance of Restoring." *Fine Arts Journal* 33, no. 5 (November 1915).

Thomas, Paul. "Midas: A Nanotechnological Exploration of Touch." *Leonardo* 42, no. 4 (2009): 186-92.

Alexandra Bischoff studies at Emily Carr University in Vancouver, British Columbia.

Exit Time

A Dialogue

Britanny Burr and Syd Peacock
Mount Royal University, Calgary, Canada

1: Is Hell other people?

2: "Could Hell be described as too much of anything without a break?"

1: *These issues of time are, at the moment, too vague.*

2: Can two people ever enter into a space of shared time?

1: *How do you mean? A space in that time flows evenly for both people, or a space in time which both people are able to enter into? Time is still too vague.*

2: Time, moments, a compilation of moments. Am I a self in relation to moments, or am I a compilation of moments into a self?

1: *Am I a time in relation to selves, or am I a self in relation to and existing in time?*

2: Am I my life, or is my life me?

1: But are we going to just ask each other questions all night and sip coffee into the moon?

2: Even when I am alone, I am existing with others.

1: Then you believe yourself to be the compilation of others. Am I talking to myself as I am here talking to you?

2: Are you really talking to me, though? You ask questions, but who will answer them? Can I really give you an answer that will satisfy? Are you talking to the other, the "other people" who make up Hell, or are you talking to a self that you are a part of? The other makes up my self; therefore, there is a contradiction for is there an(other).

1: If every self is a compilation of others, then is there a self? Is there an(other)?

2: Our immediate reactions with the world are in a manner of orientation. How are we oriented with others and/or in relation to others?

1: Isn't there a difference between existing as an orientation from or towards an(other) and affect?

2: But even the act of being born is a relation, a literal orient from someone, some (other), and you're named, and you're born a son or a daughter, but only once an(other) sees this quality of a self before the person.

1: Inez has no eyes.

2: But she is only recognized as having no eyes by Estelle, the one who cannot see her self in Inez's eyes; therefore, deeming them non-existent.

1: Garcin has eyes.

2: Estelle sees herself in his "manly" eyes. She doesn't just see herself, she finds herself. She finds her existence.

1: Then let's forget all of time that existed outside of Hell.

2: Yeah, but what's time, Syd?

1: I don't know, Brit. Check my watch.

2: Your watch? The watch that is oriented on your wrist? The watch that you can look down at and see at an angle, which I cannot? If I look at your watch, do I enter into a shared time with you?

1: God, I hope so.

2: This hallway. This is Hell?

1: It can't be. We can walk down one way, or the other, or stop, and say Hello! to a near friend, or even an enemy. We aren't stuck with each other. Our time isn't stuck with each other. We aren't in a shared time like the characters in the play. Perhaps, Hell isn't other people, but Hell is entering into a shared time with people.

2: But when the door opens, they choose to choose not to choose. And remain.

1: Yet they remain in remains. They are silenced in this moment, but not the kind of Silence that Kierkegaard holds dear. Their "choice to choose not to choose," as you say, I think, is too responsible for them. I think their lack of choice isn't a choice at all, but an avoidance of the leap of faith. They are choosing to remain with the Hell they know rather than what waits outside the door. And in this way, they are imprisoned. Their remains remain.

2: So you're saying that rather than choosing to choose not to choose, they are simply not choosing.

1: Right.

2: And the imprisonment lies in the lack of choice.

1: But not lack of choice, because the door does open. Of course, it opens, but they do not choose. They remain.

2: But they choose to remain.

1: I don't know if that can be a choice!

2: So, then, where does the Hell lie? In imprisonment? In other people? In the lack of choice, or in the choice?

1: Maybe all of the above. Let's get back to time.

2: Okay. The telling of time is my orientation.

1: So Hell is a lack of time. The eternal clock where the hands keep skipping, and you can't finish tying your shoes in time, and you never need as much time to tie your shoes.

2: Do the characters in No Exit have all the time, or no time?

1: Do we have to pick?

2: They do, don't you say?

1: I don't know. But I do know that right now I could be late for something and that only matters if there's something to be late for. But for these guys, their time moves slower in the play than the people who are still living, whom they're watching. But time isn't really moving slower for them. They don't have time. They have nothing but time.

2: So having no time is having all time. And here we are at the end of the hallway. Out of space, and out of time.

1: Right now, Brit. You and I part. There is no leap of faith for that. There is hardly even a choice. As our time flows in a direction, we part slowly. Even if you keep checking my watch, we part.

2: Exit time.

Syd Peacock currently studies English and Philosophy at Mount Royal University in Calgary, Alberta. Syd enjoys reading, writing, and visiting friends who have pets.

Britanny Burr will be graduating this spring with a Bachelor of Arts with a major in English and a minor in Philosophy from Mount Royal University in Calgary, Alberta. She enjoys creative writing, feminist philosophy, and critical theory.

Acknowledgements

AFFECTUS never would have emerged without the inspiration, dedication, and care of Ada Jaarsma, as her commitment to undergraduate Philosophy and pedagogy is truly exemplary. Ada's classes at Mount Royal University, over the last few years, have continually transformed us by way of her ability to craft a pedagogical space that is contingent—always welcoming the unanticipated. To be sure, Ada's classes have offered, and continue to offer, a space for encounters, conversations, and critical dialogues that exceed the classroom and yield great friendships, that is, friendships that became the impetus for *AFFECTUS*.

We thank Jeffrey Keshen and the Faculty of Arts as well as Jennifer Pettit, Mark Gardiner, and the Humanities Department at Mount Royal University for generously supporting this project. Amber Maader and the Students Association of Mount Royal University have ensured the success of this journal from its infancy. Without Amber's guidance and hard work, we would not have had the time or space to actualize this journal.

We thank Yana Matusovski for providing us with her artwork for this issue's cover. We extend our gratitude to Stan Dmytruk for his wonderful work on designing this issue's cover.

Many thanks to Kit Dobson, Yaw Asante, Michael Truscello, Ivan Grabovac, Randy Schroeder, and Alain Morin for their conversation, support, and encouragement.

JoAnne Kinaschuk's tenacity, patience, and organizational expertise during the submission process was incredibly helpful, as she received and organized all of our submissions.

Tyler Graham at Concordia University kindly looked over and translated passages from French to English for this issue, and we are thankful for his time.

Jeff Ray assiduously worked on the design for this issue since early August 2013, and his labour, skill, and talent is greatly appreciated. We thank Lisa Guenther at Vanderbilt University for graciously agreeing to participate in an interview for the inaugural issue. We thank Chloë Taylor and Catherine Clune-

Taylor at the University of Alberta for their astounding generosity in agreeing to speak at the *AFFECTUS* launch party. Lisa, Chloë, and Catherine made the time and effort to fit us into their very busy schedules, and we are grateful, privileged, and honoured to engage with them.

This journal is a product of undergraduate work. Undergraduates adjudicated, submitted, designed, proofread, reviewed, and edited. We thank all of the undergraduates involved in the production of this journal, especially the undergraduates who were thoughtful enough to consider submitting to *AFFECTUS*.

AFFECTUS COLLECTIVE

Connor Bell, University of Calgary
Diane Dang-Vu, Mount Royal University
Jeff Ray, Mount Royal University
Joel Farris, Alberta College of Art and Design
Jonathan Nash, Mount Royal University
Kaitlin Rothberger, Athabasca University
Kyle Kinaschuk, Mount Royal University
Laura Grant, Mount Royal University
Mariel Layson, Mount Royal University
Martin Matovich, University of Calgary
Mary Stephensen, University of Calgary
Matatha Barr, Mount Royal University
Michael Giesbrecht, Concordia University
Mike Thorn, Mount Royal University
Miriam Bronski, University of Calgary
Rohan Ghatage, Mount Royal University
Sam Reid, University of Calgary
Samara Burns, University of Calgary
Syd Peacock, Mount Royal University
Tomas Boudreau, Mount Royal University
Walter Reid, University of Calgary